"Few financial advisors have effective websites, ... ve an effective social media presence. Webvisor: The Financial Advisor's Guide to the Internet should help alter the status quo. It is filled with practical, actionable advice about how to leverage the Internet to build your practice and better serve your clients"

Joel P. Bruckenstein, CFP®
Co-Chair of the Technology Tools for Today (T3) Conference
Technology Expert, Consultant, Speaker
www.joelbruckenstein.com

"The Web is irreversibly changing the way financial advisors market, connect, and interact with clients and prospects. Webvisor cuts through the clutter and jargon to deliver a clear, concise guide advisors can follow to achieve more success in today's digital world."

Bill Winterberg, CFP®
Technology Columnist, Morningstar Advisor
Principal of FPPad.com

"Webvisor provides a comprehensive and concise blueprint for any financial advisor that is looking to develop or enhance their digital (on-line) strategy."

Victor Gaxiola
Social Media Strategist
www.red7marketing.com

webvisor

The Financial Advisor's
Guide To The Internet

By Bart Wisniowski & Jason Lindstrom

Cover design: courtesy of Catalin Negraru of
www.design4advisors.com

Cartoonist: Rob Cottingham of www.SocialSignal.com

Editor: Richard Best

ISBN: 1460917863

ISBN-13: 9781460917862

DEDICATION

This book is dedicated to our families, friends,
colleagues and clients that have supported
us in our journey.
Thank you for believing in us!

CONTENTS

Acknowledgments   ix

Introduction   xiii

CHAPTER 1   Overview   1

CHAPTER 2   Creating a Website   17

CHAPTER 3   Social Media: Is It Hype or Hyper-Marketing?   33

CHAPTER 4   Newsletter/Email Marketing   51

CHAPTER 5   To Blog or Not to Blog   59

CHAPTER 6   On the Web, Content is King   69

CHAPTER 7   Marketing Your Website   83

CHAPTER 8   Monitoring and Measuring for Results   99

CHAPTER 9   You and the Web – The New Compliance Frontier   109

Conclusion   115

ACKNOWLEDGEMENTS

Putting together this book was an interesting project. We really enjoyed working with our partners, our clients, contributors and numerous individuals in the financial services industry. And like with every new type of project, we also learned a thing or two.

We'd like to thank the following special people who helped make this book possible:

Our entire team at AdvisorWebsites.com but especially Todd, Woojun, James, Ryan, Alex, Lisa and Kevin. We really appreciate your help in so many areas of this project while still working extremely hard to keep our clients happy.

A special big thank you to our colleague Loic Jeanjean who was instrumental in shaping this book and the content that would be included. Loic is the director of Sales and Web Marketing at Advisor Websites and having his ideas and blog posts simplified the entire process for us.

To Bart's wife Darcey, for her support and being the creative behind the book title, Bart's parents and sister, and his "little guy" for giving him very enjoyable breaks during the writing process.

To Jason's wife Opi and his parents for their unconditional support.

And then comes our editor Richard Best. He read our drafts, understood our message, and helped us say what we wanted to say. Thank you.

Finally, we need to thank Stephen Jagger for all of his support and advice on how to go about writing your first book. We're glad you did it first!

FOREWORD

When there is no understanding, there is judgment. When there is judgment, there can be no understanding.

Like the Chinese Proverb that states, "I hear and I forget; I see and I remember; I do and I understand" ... WebVisor – The Financial Advisor's Guide To The Internet, will cause financial advisors to understand and capitalize on the internet & social media through reading the thought leading information, and through the completion of the exercises that are at the end of each chapter.

There are some financial advisors that scoff and ridicule the benefits of the internet & social media and this is because they don't understand.

An absence of understanding the internet & social media is like accompanying your best high net worth client to an awards dinner where they are the guest of honor.... and you forget to bring your business cards.

The internet & social media are just like an event. You don't go around flogging your business cards, but just like being visible on the internet & social media, you present your business card to those that visit you for one.

Understanding the internet & social media is about understanding that it isn't about what you are going to get from the internet & social media, it is about understanding that with all relationships, it is about the value that you bring to the relationships that you serve.

Financial advisors will be better positioned to meet and exceed their sales goals with the support of the internet & social media through their actions that will be inspired by the value added new thought leading understanding from WebVisor – The Financial Advisor's Guide To The Internet.

Simon Reilly
Coach, Speaker, Writer
www.leadingadvisor.com

INTRODUCTION

"The Internet? We are not interested in it."

- Bill Gates, 1993

If you are a financial advisor, you probably remember exactly where you were just before 3 P.M. on the 6th of May in 2010, the moment when the Dow began its spine chilling, 20 minute plunge of 1000 points. As you watched your computer screen in stunned horror, a tsunami of data bits was unleashed that blanketed the globe within seconds after the markets began to plummet. In an instant, more than 200 million people were frozen in their place as they witnessed the unprecedented financial calamity, and then breathe a collective sigh of relief in the ensuing minutes as the market recovered most of its loss. It would be a while after the market had recovered that the major media outlets would report on the event.

By the time you logged off for the day, most of your clients already knew of the event. Chances are they were one of the 200 million people who saw the live stream of posts as the event unfolded on Twitter or Facebook[1], or they were a recipient of one of millions of shared links that flowed into email inboxes that day. They could have also delivered one of the nearly 5 million Google search hits that "1000 point drop"

---

1   Estimated number of world-wide internet users logged into social media and micro-blog sites at any one time based on Forrester Social Media Research.

received and returned almost 2 million search results*[2] for news, updates, and insight on the event.

Question: How soon after the events of May 6th did all of your clients hear from you and how did you communicate with them? If you think that the answer is insignificant, because after all, that is in the past and things are going more smoothly now, then read on. You may be missing the mark completely.

Your Clients Live in the New Digital World

A decade ago, in the aftermath of 9/11, the 24-hour news cycle spawned by the cable news networks, quickly emerged which accelerated the decline of the major news networks and print media as the predominant sources of news. As the internet became more ubiquitous, and eventually gave birth to Web 2.0, the public has gradually adapted websites, social media and the blogosphere as its principle news sources.

Today, approximately 80% of Americans, from Gen Y to early Boomers, are active internet users, and 75% of the total group of users, prefer to obtain their enlightenment from the Web[3]. Their primary Web destinations for news and insight? Websites, Blogs and the social networks, by a huge margin. It seems that those who wish to be more informed no longer trust the muddled sound bites offered in the main stream news, and have come to rely upon those they do trust: their community of friends in their social networks.[4]

---

2   Estimate using Google Analytics for search term "1000 point drop" on May 6, 2010

3   2009 Razorfish Digital Brand Experience Study http://feed.razorfish.com/feed09/the-data/

4   According to a CNN report on a Pew research study, "Seventy-five percent of respondents said they get news forwarded through e-mail or posts on social networking sites, while 37 percent of online users said they've reported news, commented on a story or shared it on sites like Facebook and Twitter, the survey said." (CNN. *Survey: More Americans get news from Internet than newspapers or radio.* Web. September 2010)

The informed people of today want to engage and interact with their information sources, which may explain why, in just the last few years, the internet has eclipsed television as the medium that most Americans rely upon for all forms of news, information and entertainment[5]. From all of this, one can only surmise that, if it doesn't exist in digital space, it is more likely to be disregarded, distrusted, or deemed insignificant by the majority of Americans. What a difference a decade makes.

The way this new mindset translates to the decision-making or purchasing behavior of consumers should be of particular interest to financial advisors, who are struggling with how to develop an effective marketing strategy. In their book, *Sociable!*, Shane Gibson and Stephen Jagger encapsulate the evolving purchasing behavior of consumers this way:

> *The traditional approach to marketing is to say, "I need to control the message. I need to build a fence, a gate, and a lock around my data base. I am going to push my email at you when I want to, you are going to read the information that I want you to read, and you are going to discuss it only by submitting comments that I approve." The marketer or sales person used to control how we experienced their brands, products and services in the sales processes. This approach no longer works. People don't want to fill in their information on a site to learn about us. Your database is basically alive now. They choose whether or not they are going to learn about us. Furthermore, they choose how they are going to learn. They also choose when they will do so. It's on their timeline.*

---

5   Lee Rainie,Director, Pew Internet & American Life Project "How the Internet is Changing Consumer Behavior and Expectations". Speech to SOCAP Symposium. .Washington, DC. May 2006

Getting in Step

With all of that as a backdrop, the question for you as a financial advisor is, "Are you prepared to survive, compete and thrive in a digitally connected world where the expectation of instant and constant communication is the minimum standard by which all professional services are measured?"

The first step is to recognize that the Web is the new seat of information and knowledge power and then take the incremental steps to moving towards the digital world that resides there. David Drucker, an independent financial advisor since 1981, industry author and speaker, addresses this first hurdle that advisors need to clear:

> *"It all starts with the electronic world around us. We use these new communication tools every day when we click a website link that plays a video, or when we read an e-zine received by e-mail, or when we make a new connection on www.LinkedIn.com (or any other social-or-business-networking website). What most of us don't do, though, is take the next logical step, which is to appreciate the power of these tools, first, and find out how to incorporate them into our own communications, second."*
> **David Drucker, Keeping the Lines Open,**
> *Financial Planning Magazine.* **Aug 2008**

The Value of *WebVisor*
– The financial advisors guide to the internet

This book is not intended to be an all-inclusive "how to" for building an effective web presence. Rather, it is a blueprint, filled with ideas, basic formulas, and resources to facilitate a brainstorm for developing your own web strategy. Our goal was to provide you with a concise and succinct read. This book is to be used during the critical phase of envisioning and planning, which when done extensively, can save you an enormous amount of time, effort and money in the actual implementation of your strategy.

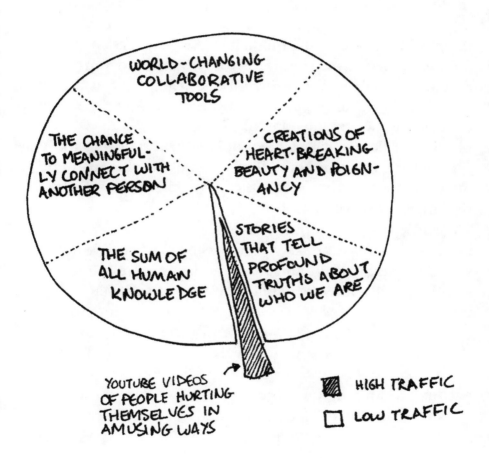

What's on the web vs. how we use the web

In the chapters to follow you will begin to develop the "big picture" of how your web strategy will transform your marketing, increase your visibility, enhance your relationships, and position you as a client-centric, trusted financial professional who merits the attention of a digitally connected market.

In Chapter 1, the basic building blocks of a complete web strategy are outlined followed by more detailed explanations in Chapters 2 through 6 of how to create and implement them in the context of a financial advisory practice. Chapter 7 focuses on the marketing of your brand and your website employing your web platform tools. Chapter 8 is a primer on monitoring and measuring your platform in order to achieve the best results. Finally, Chapter 9 discusses the 800 pound gorilla in the room, compliance, and how to navigate the evolving rules and guidelines for web marketing, in other words, addresses the question of "Can this web stuff work in the financial services industry?".

WebVisor – The financial advisors guide to the internet, while not all-encompassing – It can't possibly be because the technology is highly fluid and new standards are emerging constantly - is still a must-read before investing valuable resources into creating your web presence. Whether you intend to proceed on a do-it-yourself basis or enlist the services of experts, this book will provide you with the essential knowledge and understanding of how a web strategy will connect you with an ever-expanding digital world.

Ray Adamson, a leading industry expert on best practices for financial advisors, frames the value of *WebVisor* this way:

> *Optimizing (working at the highest level of your ability on the activities that give you the biggest reward) is only possible when you employ leverage. In business leverage means employing people and technology to do the things that you don't want to do; the things that don't*

make sense for you to do; or to do things on a wider scale than you could do on your own. The focus of this book is leveraging the internet and Social Media in order to grow your business profitably. Your challenge is to clarify your marketing strategy and this book will help you do this.

Web Resource

In conjunction with this publication, we encourage the reader to reference our educational and dynamic blog where you may find a large variety of posts ranging in topics from sample templates, marketing ideas and case studies, advanced SEO techniques, technology provider spotlights, guest contributors and anything in between. Our blog is available to anyone free of charge at www.advisorwebsites.com/blog

Chapter Exercises

Lastly, we try to end off each chapter with a couple of easy exercises that you can perform to get you going on your internet journey!

1 OVERVIEW

"I must confess that I've never trusted the Web. I've always seen it as a coward's tool. Where does it live? How do you hold it personally responsible? Can you put a distributed network of fiber-optic cable "on notice"? And is it male or female? In other words, can I challenge it to a fight?"

- Stephen Colbert - comedian

Few people today would argue that the internet has not significantly changed the way they conduct their lives. In just a few short years their interaction with the internet has evolved from a relationship of convenience to an emotional and economic dependency that has forever changed the way they make everyday decisions. The digital influence of the web now surpasses all other forms of persuasion, including TV and print advertising, and even peer influence[6]. The question business marketers should ask themselves today is, "What kind of digital influence do we have over our market?"

Have you been online today? It would be difficult to imagine that, as a financial advisor, you haven't been speeding down the

---

6   Lee Rainie, Director, Pew Internet & American Life Project, "How the Internet is Changing Consumer Behavior and Expectations". Speech to SOCAP Symposium. Washington, DC May 2006

information highway at some point today, searching, researching, comparing, shopping, or validating. But even if you haven't, you can be sure that your clients and prospects have been doing so. In their 2010 Digital Future Study, USC researchers found that Americans spend an average of 19 hours a week on the internet, and at least two of those hours are devoted to their personal finances[7].

During the recession of 2008 – 2009, the internet reached a new level of influence as a key source of solutions for the economic woes suffered by the connected public. More than two-thirds of American adults accessed the internet in search of relief from their financial difficulties brought about by the lingering recession. For most Americans, the internet has moved beyond its utility as a decision-making tool and has become their go-to resource for problem-solving.

Are You Invisible to Your Market?

If, as most of the research indicates, the internet has become the core decision-making tool for consumers, it would suggest that financial advisors who do not incorporate a web strategy into their marketing efforts are far less likely to gain any significant mind-share of their market. Frankly, it is more likely that they may be completely invisible to their market. To put it in more blunt terms: Avoid the web and your phone may stop ringing.

Having a web presence is a validation of your business, much like the business card or brochure was a decade ago. You might remember a time when you introduced yourself to someone as a "financial advisor," yet you had no business card to present. You may have felt an uncomfortable sense of inadequacy, along with some paranoia that the person may have questioned your legitimacy.

---

7   The Center for the Digital Future at the USC Annenberg School *www.digitalcenter.org/pdf/2010_digital_future_final_release.pdf*

Today, simply presenting a business card no longer suffices as a way for consumers to validate you as an authority in your profession. Websites have become the new calling card without which your legitimacy may very well come into question.

The Internet's Influence on Purchasing Behavior

All we have to do is think back on some of the major purchase decisions that we made in our lives to fully appreciate the true impact the internet has had on our purchasing behavior.

Boy, get your coat! We're buying a TV!
(A note from Bart Wisniowski…)

One of my more vivid memories is the day our family purchased a brand new television set. Although my dad had been thinking about getting one for a while, he seemed surprisingly impulsive when he jumped up and shouted, "Boy, get your coat! We're buying a TV!"

Maybe it was because I was a young kid, but the thing that really stood out for me that day was the enormity of the process. We began our search in the morning at a television store, and then bounced between department stores and electronic stores. In the span of a rainy Vancouver Saturday, we must have visited six or seven different stores and heard as many sales pitches. Finally, at the end of a long day, our family drove home with a brand new Magnavox color television set.

22 Years Later….

Flash forward to 2010. On a routine visit to my parents, right around the time of the winter Olympics, I noticed that the trusty old Magnavox I grew up with was gone, and in its place was a brand new 50-inch flat screen TV. Thinking back to the major production involved in the last TV purchase, I hesitated to ask my dad how it went this time. He shrugged and told me he just ran down to Costco after he saw a sales promotion on their website.

My dad is not the kind of person to comb the internet for sales promotions, so I pressed him some more. He told me that he had received an email newsletter from Costco, promoting a new toolset he was interested in buying, and that when he clicked through to the website, he saw a link to the television promotion and clicked through. He then clicked around to compare products and prices, and two hours later, he was installing his new television set.

Aside from the fact that his second TV purchase involved substantially less time, effort and bloviating from commissioned sales reps, it became strikingly clear that my dad's use of the internet triggered a complete evolution in his purchasing behavior. Unlike his first big purchase, when he made a laborious effort to go out and find a TV, this time, the TV found him! And, because he had instant access to all the information he needed, he had made his purchase decision before he started his car.

It was then that I concluded that the influence of the internet was going to eliminate a lot of childhood memories of those big family purchases. More important, I realized that the internet is a transformational force that will ultimately determine who the winners and losers will be in the business arena.

A Web Presence = Trust, Credibility

The internet has shrunk the financial world and made it more transparent, which has increased consumers' access to information that was once only available through financial institutions or financial professionals. For the first time, a majority of people now conduct their basic banking activities online and most of them have made the quality of online access their primary criteria for choosing a banking institution. The explosion of investors who have taken up online trading in the last decade has become legendary in the short history of the internet.

More significantly for financial advisors, the vast majority of the mass affluent spend as much as 65%[8] of their time on the internet gathering information on products and services as part of their decision-making process. For people with incomes over $150,000, the number should be changed from 65% to 85%.[9] In the context of their personal finances, investors search for information, advice and tips that will help them formulate financial decisions. They look to websites, blogs and social media sites such as LinkedIn, Twitter, Facebook, and even YouTube, in pursuit of financial knowledge.

The good news for financial advisors is that most of these investors will still look to them in order to validate their information and findings. These "validators" are perfectly fine roaming the internet cloud for their own edification and then relying upon a trusted advisor to help close their decision-making loop. The bad news is that, if their advisor is not as digitally connected or web-savvy as they are, they may decide to look elsewhere.

One of the quickest ways to lose client's trust is to fail to form a bond based on the way they like to communicate. The really big news for advisors is that a growing number of affluent investors prefer to interact with their advisors through the internet, either through social media sites or interactive

8   Pew Internet. *Use of the internet in higher-income households* http://pewinternet.org/Reports/2010/Better-off-households/Report/Highest-earning-households.aspx November 2010

9   Pew Internet. *Use of the internet in higher-income households* http://pewinternet.org/Reports/2010/Better-off-households/Report/Highest-earning-households.aspx November 2010

websites. The message here is that, in order to maintain credibility and the trust of your clients, having a web presence is a virtual necessity.

A Blueprint for Getting Web-Wired

When television and print were the primary purveyors of persuasion, small businesses were at a disadvantage due to the expense of advertising with these mediums. Now the Web, as the predominant medium for consumer marketing, has leveled the playing field for small businesses so they can more easily compete with the big boys for the consumer's attention through their own web presence.

Creating an effective web presence doesn't have to be an expensive proposition. Many of the tools that can be utilized in a complete web strategy don't cost a dime, but they can be time consuming at first. In order to leverage the time and resources spent on building your web presence, it is important to consider a strategy that employs multiple tools and tactics, each linked or integrated with each other for an optimal strategy. This book focuses on four core tools:

- ✓ Website
- ✓ Social Media
- ✓ Email Marketing
- ✓ Blog

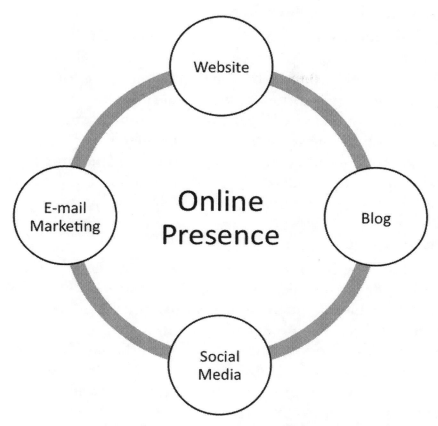

4 Components For Successful Online Presence

Website

A website should be considered as a portal into your firm and the front end of your communication with prospects and clients. A well-structured website will illuminate your profile, values, and services, and provide compelling content and resources for your target market. In the digitally connected world, your website becomes the foundation of your branding efforts and will differentiate you in a highly competitive market. It is also the central hub of your online presence, linking all of your social media tools to create an optimal presence among the search engines and greater interaction with your market.

Social Media and Networking

The internet has also spawned a revolution in the sphere of social networking. For better or for worse, social web, also known as Web 2.0, has become the dominant forum for friends and family to meet and mingle. Advisors using social media can create a bigger presence online, cement their ties to existing clients and encourage "electronic" word-of-mouth. The number of social media tools is expanding every day providing financial advisors with a number of ways to promote their brand and interact with their target markets.

Email Marketing

Email has long been the established mode of client communication, and it too has evolved into a vital marketing tool that is capable of nurturing relationships. Many financial advisors utilize CRM programs that automate the email communication process to support their marketing, sales and client service efforts. Email marketing, integrated with an automated CRM program, has become a core component of many advisors' marketing strategy.

Blogging

In addition to creating compelling web content, it is important to provide current information and updates to keep your audience engaged (and to maintain the attention of the search engines). Blogs are easy to set up and maintain, and they are an excellent way to share your message and your thought leadership while engaging your clients and prospects. It's a relationship business and blogging enables your target market to get a sense of your personality and perspective, which is what most people want when choosing a financial advisor.

Putting the Pieces Together

The big advantage of using the web as your marketing medium is that all of the tools you utilize can provide a link to each other, which can provide a path for your audience to follow. That's why they call it the "web." Independent of each other, these tools are valuable and they serve their own purpose: to raise your visibility, cultivate relationships, expand your market reach, and enhance your brand. However, collectively they work as a powerful, integrated strategy to drive the traffic to where you want it going, to your main website. This is a good place where you can convert your traffic into prospects by getting them to fill out a form, send you an email, or pick up the phone and call you. Having said that, keep in mind that conversions can also happen on social media sites, blogs and emails so make sure not to ignore those opportunities.

A CASE STUDY IN WEB SUCCESS

Private Ocean (www.privateocean.com) is one of the oldest privately-held wealth management firms in the San Francisco Bay Area. Founded by Richard Stone and Greg Friedman, the firm has over $700 million in assets under management.

They have been honored as one of the Top 100 Registered Investment Advisors (RIAs) nationwide seven times by Worth Magazine. In 2009 they were chosen by San Francisco Business Times as one of the Top 25 Independent Advisors and one of the Most Influential Advisors by Investment Advisor Magazine. The firm was also named number 4 in the San Francisco

Business Times list of Top 25 independent RIAs in 2008.

The firm prides itself on being able to provide its clients with the intimate experience of a small firm while harnessing the power and discipline of a large one.

"Everything we do is driven by the specific needs of our clients," said Friedman. "That's something a lot of firms say, but we're making it a reality."

To accomplish that, the firm has invested heavily in technology as a tool for communicating actively with clients, enhancing the degree of personal service and providing high levels of secure access to personal account information.

Their vision of creating the ultimate personalized experience for each of their clients relies extensively on a complete, multi-pronged web strategy that includes:

- ✓ Website: includes company info, products and services, client resources
- ✓ Newsletter: published monthly and archived on website
- ✓ Live webinars: scheduled regularly and archived
- ✓ Client log-in: access to secured client account data, reports, and documents
- ✓ Social media: all principles maintain an active presence on social media sites such as LinkedIn

The Private Ocean team may be on the cutting edge of web marketing for financial advisors but they are the first to recognize that there is still a lot to learn.

> **"We recognize that utilizing the various aspects of the internet in our operation has tremendous opportunity. We also realize that this is a constantly changing environment and stay very open-minded as to the types of tools and technologies that allow us to meet the evolving needs of our clients."**
>
> **Greg Friedman, President, Private Ocean**

You Need to Get Your Name Out in Front, But Watch Your Back

Building a web presence for the purpose of increasing your visibility and stature could not be any easier. Using the core tools, such as your website and social media, will enable you to promote your brand in the most favorable light. That's the good news. The bad news is that the internet is an encyclopedia of just about everything that has ever been published about any individual who has an image to protect. As easy as you have tried to make it for your prospects to find all that is good and positive about you, the internet makes it just as easy for them to uncover one of your skeletons.

Here is a scenario that illuminates the lack of control that people have over their personal information that may be floating up in the cloud and how it can influence a prospect's decision-making process:

- ✓ One of your 'A' clients is tossing back a beer with a colleague after work, and the colleague confides that he needs some help with his retirement plan.

✓ You have trained your client well, so he enthusiastically recommends your services to his colleague.

✓ You follow-up with your new prospect and agree to an initial consultation.

So far so good, until he Googles your name….

✓ Your new prospect wants to do some homework so he Googles your name.

✓ You have an effective web presence, so your website pops up near the top of his search, along with some sites with which you have a professional affiliation. Your LinkedIn, Facebook and Twitter sites follow right in a row, just as you planned.

✓ Then something else pops up. The YouTube video in which you were tagged by a buddy that highlights your championship performance at the local beer pong tournament, which you won, hands down while wearing just your underwear. OK, it may not be as bad as that, but, if your prospect continues to look on page two or three of his Google search results, who knows what he may find?

✓ You receive an email from your former prospect asking for a "postponement" of the consultation meeting.

The point is that you could spend an enormous amount of time creating a polished and professional brand only to have it completely dismantled by an errant post from your past. When building a web presence it is important to gain control over all information on your personal and professional life, past, present and future.

Know Where You're Going, or You May End Up Somewhere Else

Embarking upon a complete web strategy can be a major undertaking requiring several stages of development and a significant commitment of time and resources. A more realistic approach might be to break the strategy down into individual components that can more easily be implemented and then linked or integrated as components are added later. The key to this approach is to prioritize your goals and objectives for your web strategy. Doing so will also help you establish some benchmarks for measurement so you can assess the effectiveness of your efforts and make any necessary adjustments to your strategy.

Your own goals and priorities will be based on where you are in your business and your current state of web readiness. These are just some of the objectives we have heard from our advisor clients:

✓ Raise visibility/credibility/stature
✓ Electronic business card
✓ Provide resources and support for clients
✓ Business and lead generation
✓ Learn more about client's and prospect's needs and interests
✓ Become searchable on Google or other search engines
✓ Build a better website than their colleagues
✓ Assist in dating (seriously, one of our clients wanted a professional photo and website that he could use in conjunction with a dating site. He's now married!)

Once you have your goals and objectives defined, you can begin to implement the web components that best support them and you feel most comfortable utilizing. You will have some key measures to benchmark against and ensure that you are on track.

Monitoring and Measuring is Key to Web Success

Being a financial advisor, you understand the importance of optimizing resources for achieving maximum ROI. No matter the amount of your financial investment in your web strategy, it is important to be able to track and measure your marketing efforts in order to determine their effectiveness. The huge advantage of using the web as your marketing medium is that it provides a wealth of usage information and statistics that can easily be sifted and analyzed. Examples of available data include:

✓ Amount and quality of traffic to your sites
✓ The "stickiness" of your site (how long people stay)
✓ The usefulness of your site (repeated visits)
✓ Which content is most valuable (number of views)
✓ How your clients interact with your site (were any forms filled out?)
✓ Which external links drive the most traffic to your site

Web marketing is a dynamic process that must be able to constantly adapt and adjust to trends, changing conditions, and new opportunities. The ability to measure and analyze actual usage ensures that you will be able to make small adjustments over time as opposed to major reactionary changes that can be costly.

This book drills down more deeply on measurement and analytics in Chapter 7.

What You'll Find in the Rest of this Book

Up to this point, this book has probably confirmed much of what you already knew – that the internet is a powerful force that has transformed the way buyers and sellers interact and that if sellers don't adapt to the evolving decision-making patterns of the buyers, they will quickly become obsolete in the marketplace.

What you may not know is just how easy it really is to become web-wired so you can compete on a level playing field and leverage your marketing efforts in a way that can accelerate the growth of your business. This book will walk you through the key components that are essential to building an effective web presence and arm you with the tools and knowledge to launch you into action.

The world wide web is highly fluid and in a constant state of evolution. By working with the right tools and, when necessary, the right partners, you will be better able to stay on the cutting edge of web technology that will ensure your web presence hits the mark.

Keeping it Current

One small caveat we like to include in books of this sort is that technology, as it always has, is undergoing rapid change, and the internet, along with all of its applications seems to be traveling at Mach I. As such, it is important to note that some references to specific technologies and applications may have changed by the time you read this book. No matter, it's still a great read.

CHAPTER EXERCISE

✓ Type your name or your business name into several search engines (Try these 3: Google. com, Yahoo.com and Bing.com) and review the results you get.

✓ How do you feel about these results?

✓ Is this the information you want found and do you like what comes up.....? Are you surprised by any of the results and are they different from what you were expecting?

✓ If you were a prospect, how easy would it be to find information on you and your business?

2 CREATING A WEBSITE

"When I took office, only high energy physicists had ever heard of what is called the Worldwide Web.... now even my cat has its own page."

- Bill Clinton

Are you ready to get in the game? Creating an effective website, or improving on an existing site, doesn't have to break your marketing budget; in fact, it may help reduce the overall costs of your marketing initiatives. It can consume a lot of time, however, especially if you go down the wrong road and find yourself backtracking or changing direction to get to your destination. Financial advisors know that to achieve financial success, a clear plan based on established goals and objectives can save a substantial amount of money and time. This same fundamental principal applies to building a successful website.

This chapter lays out a series of planning steps that will set you on the right path and steer you toward a successful launch of your website. The more time you spend in the planning stage will yield bigger returns when you are ready to launch your site.

Set Your Sights

We touched on the importance of having specific goals and objectives in Chapter 1. The key to setting goals for your web strategy is to be realistic and make sure that they are measurable. While the ultimate goal of any marketing strategy should be to increase revenues, the actual measures of your marketing initiatives should be based on their specific objectives, such as increasing leads, raising brand awareness, establishing brand authority, or expanding market reach. Revenue is a direct measure of sales activities which should increase if the marketing objectives are achieved.

For instance, if your business goal is to increase your total income by improving your revenue per client, you may want to focus on establishing your brand authority and credibility, which should lead to your clients entrusting you with more of their money. This could also lead to additional client referrals, which will further improve your revenue per client ratio. Your website and social media tools will provide you with data and information that will help you link your revenue results with your marketing initiatives.

Begin with the End in Mind

As with any undertaking, it is recommended that you begin with the end in mind. Your website will have a "look and feel" that reflects your vision of how you present yourself, and it should be structured in a way that optimizes your message. The most effective websites are clean and simple, with easily accessible content and easy navigation. Your clients and prospects are looking for the right information, so it is important that they perceive your website as being the right source.

N⊙ISE TO SIGNAL
Rob Cottingham · socialsignal.com/n2s

As this next slide demonstrates, the ROI of setting fire to your money isn't quite as favorable as blowing it all at the track, but still outperforms building a Flash intro screen.

You don't need to be a web designer to create an effective website. If you start with the right vision it becomes easier to piece together the right components in a way that best embodies your brand. Because it is sometimes difficult to paint your vision from a completely blank canvas, you can use this brainstorming checklist of website components – just add your own colors.

✓ **Domain name** – This is how people will find you on the internet so it should be your most important consideration. More on domain names later in this chapter.

✓ **Professional Photo** – You will be judged by your appearance, so you may want to consider having a professional photo of yourself, your team in a group and your individual team members.

✓ **Biography** – Your biography is key to making the right connection with your target market.

✓ **Practice profile** – A description of your practice, mission, vision, product and services, contact information etc.

✓ **Resources for your website** – The content of your website is the key determinant in how many visitors your site attracts and how often they come back, so it is important that it be informative, relevant, and timely information. Content resources include timely articles, newsletters, blog posts, tools such as calculators, client portal links and educational materials.

✓ **Imagery** – Your website imagery will complete the "look and feel" of your website, and it is a key element in your branding. We find that most advisors whom we have worked with will choose one of two approaches, or a combination of both:

    ✓ **Geographic** – If you work primarily within a geographic region such as a city, state, province etc. you may want to use images throughout your website that link your brand with a location. This will help your visitors connect with you from a geographic standpoint.

    ✓ **Lifestyle** – Some advisors choose to use market specific imagery that connects them to their target market. For example, if you primarily work with doctors you may want to include images of medical professionals and locations. Attorneys – a courtroom, legal images, etc... Business Owners – a board room, brick and mortar locations, handshakes etc.

✓ **Additional look and feel considerations** – Depending on your type of practice, you may need to adhere to certain graphic standards and apply specific logos. As you consider the overall layout of your site, including colors, font type, page structure, etc., it's best to look at other sites to get ideas. Bookmark three or four sites that appeal to you.

✓ **Compliance process** – Before you brainstorm too much, it's important to check in with your compliance department. Most broker-dealers allow advisors to have their own website, however, each has its own specifications for building a compliant website. Some will provide an approved template while others have a detailed do's and don'ts list. Your website will probably have to contain all of the disclosure language as prescribed by your compliance department.

✓ **Testimonials** – These help to build credibility and people do read them. There may be a compliance issue in their use, so check with your compliance department. Rule of Thumb:

  ✓ USA → Testimonials <u>not</u> Allowed
  ✓ Canada → Testimonials Allowed

✓ **Social media considerations** – There is no doubt that social media is a major force in web marketing, and it would be a huge mistake not to incorporate it into your web strategy. Because most social media sites are built on Web 2.0 platforms, they can be easily integrated with your website, providing more opportunities for cross promotion and attracting more visitors to your site. You should begin looking into such social media sites as LinkedIn, Facebook, Twitter, and even YouTube. Be sure to check with your compliance department for their guidelines on the use of these sites.

✓ **Integration** – As an advisor, you likely leverage technology solutions for various aspects of your business with some of the many providers out there (CRM's, Client Portals, Calculators etc.). We have noticed that many of these providers are starting to be more "Web Friendly" making these solutions work quite well with your website.

✓ **Choose a reputable provider** – Choosing the right provider can make all the difference as to whether your website project is a success or failure. Make sure your provider understands the financial services industry and the compliance issues. A good provider acts more like a partner in your web strategy, helping you to customize your website based on your vision. Leverage their expertise and consider any advice they give you.

It's All in the Name

There is, perhaps, no more important step than the first one which is to name your domain. Your domain name, becomes your identifier or address on the internet. It also becomes the front end of your brand because it is the way the search engines and your market will be able to find you. So, it is important to give this critical step the time and attention it needs to get it right the first time.

Your domain name is the core of your URL address, which is what people will type into the address line of their browser. Here's an example of a URL address:

www.bartwisniowski.com

- ✓ **"www"** – this stands for World Wide Web.
- ✓ **"bartwisniowski"** – your actual domain name as one word.
- ✓ **".com"** – this is referred to as the Top Level Domain (TLD). Common TLDs include .com, .biz, .org, .net, .info. Geographic versions are also available and may include .us, .ca, .co.uk, .eu, etc.

Putting together all components, separated by periods, gives you your website address.

Choosing Your Domain Name

- ✓ **Brainstorm** – jot down your top five desired names.
- ✓ **Short and easy** –the shorter your domain name the better. Five to 20 characters is ideal. Remember, your visitors may have to type this into their browser. Here are a couple of ways to keep your domain name short:

  - ✓ Use initials to shorten long names. (i.e. instead of using www.**wilkinsonsmithmichaelsfinanicial**.com, you can go with www.**wsmfinancial**.com)
  - ✓ We have seen the word "Financial Services" abbreviated. (i.e., instead of using www.**simpsonfinancialservicesincorporated**.com, you can go with www.**simpsonfs**.com)

- ✓ **Tricky spellings** – be careful of tricky spellings.
- ✓ **Easy to remember** – the easier the better. Full names are easier to remember than initials or abbreviations.

✓ **Your name vs. firm name** - Typically most advisors will either choose their personal name (i.e. www.**firstlast**.com) or a firm name (i.e. www.**smithfinancial**.com). **TIP:** Register both names. Your advisor website can have more than one domain name if you wish. Typing either domain name will take your visitors to your website, but you will have to choose a primary one.

Choosing Your Top Level Domain

Domain names include the Top Level Domain (TLD). The most popular TLDs include **.com, .biz, .org, .net, .info**. Geographic versions are also available and may include **.us, .ca, .co, .uk, .eu,** etc.

Options and observations - these can vary from individual to individual.

✓ The ".com" TLD is preferred by most. We typically recommend getting the ".com" version of the domain name if available.
✓ If .com is not available, these TLD's can be used: .net, .biz, .info, .org.
✓ The Geographic TLD can also be a very good option. i.e., .us (USA), .ca (Canada), .co.uk (United Kingdom) etc... depending where your business is based. Note: you may need to be a resident in the country in order to be able to register the geographic TLD.
✓ It is recommended that you register all of the main TLDs in order to prevent others from "stealing" your domain name. Remember you can have more than one domain name pointed to your website.

Once you have chosen a couple of options, you will need to check to see if your desired domain name is available. To see if a domain name is available you can use any domain name provider such as www.GoDaddy.com.

What if the Domain Name I Want is Taken?

If your personal or company name is very common or a popular one, it may be taken, and you will not be able to register it. At this point you have a few options.

- ✓ **Try a different TLD** (i.e., .com version is taken, you can try the .net, .biz, .us etc…)
- ✓ **Try adding a hyphen** (although this is not an ideal solution, it is more likely to be available).
- ✓ **Contact the domain name owner** to see if you could buy the domain name from them. Note, this can be a very long, painful and expensive process. Some registrars provide this as a service for a fee. You should proceed with an alternate version of the domain name in the meantime.
- ✓ **You can wait** for the domain name to expire and try to purchase it then. Again the probability of actually getting the domain name may not be in your favor. Most businesses are not willing to let their domain names go.

More Helpful Tips!

- ✓ **Length of time** – Ideally, you want to register your domain name for as long a period as you can. This eliminates the need to manage the renewal process and the search engines like sites that aren't set to expire.
- ✓ **Choose a reliable supplier** – There are many domain name suppliers and pricing is very competitive. It is important to use a reliable company so that you'll have the necessary support in managing your domain name.

TEN QUICK TIPS FOR A SUCCESSFUL WEBSITE PHOTO

1. **For best quality**, use a professional photographer. They know how to bring the best out in anyone.
2. **Usage:** Let your photographer know that this photo will be used on a website, and possibly on other marketing collateral.
3. **Photo style:** be creative… we've seen advisors use a variety of poses and zoom levels. The most common ones include head shot, elbows and above, or waist and above. This is a personal preference so choose a pose and zoom level that accentuates your best qualities.
4. **Source file:** Provide a high quality electronic source file to your website professional (Scanned photos will naturally lose some quality during the scanning process). Although your website provider will likely shrink and edit your file, working with a high-quality source file will produce a higher quality end product.
5. **Touch ups:** your photographer or website professional should be able to do some minor touch ups in case you get a blemish on photo day.
6. **Team photos:** we encourage a great team photo, but also have individual photos done as well since team members change.
7. **File details:**
   a. 300 DPI or higher.
   b. JPEG or JPG formats work best for web.
   c. TIF format can also provide a great end product.
8. **Copyright:** make sure you own the rights to your photo for your desired use. If you are using a professional photographer, you may want to verify copyright information with them.

9. **Use a clean backdrop**, especially if you want your photo cut out and used in a banner.

10. **Dress appropriately for your target market**. Remember, your photo is often the first impressions your clients will have of you.

Putting Your Best Face Forward

First impressions are everything. Internet users have very short attention spans, and they are especially discerning when it comes to appearances, which is why the "look and feel" of your website is so critical. Studies have shown that when a personal image is displayed, it creates an opportunity for the visitor to make a personal connection and stay on the site a little longer. Obviously, as a financial services professional, the way you present yourself to your clients and prospects is very important.

Make Your Website Search Engine Friendly

Simply having a web address with a website residing there doesn't ensure that anyone will be able to find it. Certainly those to whom you have provided your web address will be able to find you. The whole idea of having a website is to attract the throngs of people who don't have your web address but are on the internet searching for financial solutions. They will use the search engines, such as Google and Yahoo, to find websites that have the most relevance to the search terms they used.

Search Engine Optimization is the technical side of web marketing that does require at least some basic understanding of how search engines do their work. The subject of SEO can take up volumes of books to explain, and companies pay SEO experts thousands of dollars to optimize their websites.

The key point to take away is that a website needs to be created with the search engines in mind. Some would refer to it as "search engine friendly", making your website easy for the search engines to find.

These are some of the key SEO techniques that web novices can utilize when designing their website:

Page Title: The page title, which is what appears in the browser window when viewing a web page, is what the search engines see when they visit your site. It is also the first place they look for relevant keywords that are used to match with a search request. It is important for the page title to contain the keywords that people are most likely going to use in their search terms. The title shouldn't be too long (less than 70 characters) and it should mostly consist of the keywords. Each page of your website should have a distinct page title with different key words in the title.

Content: Content is key when it comes to search engines. Your content should be of high quality and it should contain relevant keywords throughout. You will not rank well for a term that is not included in your content.

Relevant Links to your website: the more relevant links to your website from respectable websites, the better chance you have. Links from your Social Media sites count!

Meta Description: The meta description is important because it contains the text that often shows up as a description in the search results. Although it is not important for optimization, it allows the searcher to see some highlights of your page. Using the right keywords in your meta description could get the searcher's attention as they scroll through the results.

Headings: Headings are the larger lines of text that introduce a page or a section of content. Your headings are important because they get the attention of the search engines, so they should contain keywords or variations of the keywords. Main headings are identified in HTML code as <h1> and they should only be used once. Sub-headings (<h2>, <h3>) should contain keywords and should be used to break up a lengthy page.

Images: Using images and graphics on your web pages can make them more attractive but in doing so, it could bog down the load speed of the page and distract the search engine bots in their search for relevant keywords. If you use images, and you should, it is important to associate some text keywords to them.

Domain Commitment: Search engines are more apt to favor websites that plan to be around for awhile. When you register your domain you should commit to at least a couple of years. 5+ years is ideal. That is indication that your site is the real deal and not some spam site.

Important Tip: Although we emphasized the importance of keywords usage on your web pages, it is very important not to go overboard. Search engines are turned off by 'keyword stuffing' which will hurt your page ranking.

Summary

As with most technological endeavors, the more time and money invested doesn't always translate to immediate success. As fast as the tools and applications are changing in the web world, trial and error, along with a little patience is what results in the biggest advancements. But, for those looking for the quickest ROI, it may pay to hire an expert who can guide you through the thought process and then have you wired for the web within a matter of days or weeks.

Working with a web developer can also ensure that your website is optimized for the best results, and that it is keeping current with the latest advancements and trends in web marketing. Because you work in a specialized, and compliance-driven niche, firms such as Advisor Websites (www.advisorwebsites.com) that concentrate on web development for financial advisors may be the best solution.

CHAPTER EXERCISE

✓ Contact your compliance department and see if you are allowed to have a website. If yes, ask them for any guidelines or considerations to keep in mind.

✓ Find and jot down 3-4 websites you really like. These could be those of your colleagues, competitors or completely unrelated to your industry but should give you a good idea of the kind of things you like / dislike. (what do you like about the site i.e. look and feel, content, functionality, imagery etc…)

✓ If you have not already done so, this may be a good time to secure your own domain name. You can secure your domain name from any reputable domain name provider like www.GoDaddy.com or domains.advisorwebsites.com

3 SOCIAL MEDIA: IS IT HYPE OR HYPER-MARKETING?

"LinkedIn is for people you know. Facebook is for people you used to know. Twitter is for people you want to know."

- Author Unknown

Recently, nothing has garnered more attention in the World Wide Web than the phenomenon of social media and its influence on the way people congregate and communicate. With hundreds of millions of people digitally connected through social networks, the world has suddenly become a cyber community no bigger than the size of a computer screen. In addition to radically changing the social mores of relationships and networking, it has transformed the way in which businesses market to their constituencies and build their brand.

Financial Advisors in Social Media – Better Late than Never

While financial advisors have been slow to adopt social media, largely due to compliance and regulatory ambiguities, they are quickly discovering the powerful attraction that it holds for their target markets and its potential as a business development tool. In a recent study, it showed that 60% of financial advisors are actively using social media and that half of those users reported receiving quality referrals as a result of their use. Another survey showed that financial advisors believe that social media is second only to face-to-face opportunities for establishing and cultivating new relationships[10].

Financial advisors are learning what other businesses have known for a while, and that is that social media has become one of the most effective and efficient ways to build their brand and get their message out to their target market. Here's what business users say are the top benefits of their social media use:

Top Ways Small Businesses Benefit from Social Media[11]	
Generate exposure for my business	85%
Increased traffic / subscribers on my site	63%
Resulted in new business partnerships	56%
Helped us rise in the search engines	54%
Generated quality leads	52%
Helped to sell products /close business	48%
Reduced overall marketing expenses	42%

This Bank CEO Walks the Walk

In their book, *Sociable! How Social Media is Turning Sales and Marketing Upside Down*, Shane Gibson and Stephen Jagger describe their encounter with the CEO of ING Direct, who

---

10 Olivia Glauberzon, "Social media a hit with advisors". Investment Executive. (Web. Sep. 2008)

11 Michael Steltzner, Social Media Marketing Industry Report. (Web Mar 2009)

has, himself, fully adapted social media as a business strategy to support his company's commitment to customer service through transparency and engagement. The authors first "met" Peter Aceto on Twitter, where he actively posts his thoughts, insights and interacts directly with any of the 4000+ customers and staff who follow him there.

With Shane and Stephen scheduled to visit Toronto for a speaking engagement, the authors, who had been developing a relationship with Peter on Twitter, invited him to dinner for an opportunity to interview him for their book. Peter accepted. What struck the authors as remarkable was not the idea that a CEO of a $24 billion international banking institution would take time out of his busy schedule to meet with them, but that Peter, who tweets regularly about the significance of engaging with people through social media, actually walks the walk.

They asked Peter what he Tweets about and he said, "Its mostly personal, I want it to be a close representation of who I am, what I am doing to engage my staff and customers." As evidenced by a visit to his Twitter site www.Twitter.com/CEO_INGDIRECT, Peter tweets throughout the day on his views on leadership, boardroom activities, thoughts about life, and even family activities.

Peter has embraced the full social media spectrum with a presence on Facebook and YouTube, and he even has his own blog site, *Direct Talk with Peter Aceto*, in which he actively posts his more extensive thoughts and insights on financial issues of the day. Recently he blogged about the importance of social media in business, particularly his business, and he had this to say:

> *"I'm not sure that we all fully comprehend the direct relationship between social media and return on investment ("ROI") yet - a question I am often asked. But what I do*

> know is that social media has the capability to be the ulti-
> mate equalizer in commerce."

The one thing that is certain in the mind of Peter Aceto is that social media has become the central conduit that connects people and their views, and it is the dominant force of change in society today.

Social Media Etiquette: Keep it Social

As easy as it is to get connected in social media, it is just as easy to tarnish your reputation and chase followers, friends and fans away. In the short period of time that social media has existed, a social etiquette has evolved that guides the discourse and is self-policed through the various mechanisms for "un-friending" or "de-following". This is especially true for business accounts that become too overbearing in their attempts to push their products or brand.

Social media sites such as Facebook and Twitter are cyber networks or communities where people gather to meet their friends, share thoughts, and build new relationships on a social level. For those with the ultimate aim of promoting their business, the accepted approach is to keep it social at first, listen a lot, and then begin to add value to the conversation. The key with this approach is to build trust and position yourself as a thought leader and a resource who people will want to follow.

It's not much different than holding the attention of a small group of people at a social function with interesting and witty conversation and then watching the group expand as others join in. It can be a slow process as business development goes, but it's an unparalleled opportunity to get to know your prospects and clients on a more personal level, and vice versa, which can lead to stronger and more profitable business relationships.

The Social Media Landscape

We recognize that many financial advisors may be constrained by company policies as to which social media sites they can use. Although the number of social media sites is continuing to grow, most advisors are zeroed in on the big three: LinkedIn, Facebook, and Twitter. Even with this narrow list, getting tapped into their networks can be a little overwhelming, so we offer a brief overview of each and some tips for getting the most out of your social media efforts. Once you have finished reading this chapter we encourage you to visit the Advisor Websites blog (www.advisorwebsites.com/blog) for a number of good articles, samples, templates, case studies etc. specifically geared for financial advisors ranging from basics to advanced and choose the resources most applicable to you.

Facebook

We'll start with Facebook because it is, hands down, the most popular of all of the social media sites. With over 500 million users, it's a marketer's dream. Chances are you have your own personal Facebook page, but what about a Facebook page for your business? As with any social setting, it's never a great idea to mix business with personal interaction, and the same social etiquette applies to Facebook. Plus, you probably don't want your clients and prospects to follow your progress on Mafia Wars. By creating a separate business page, you have the opportunity to introduce yourself as a business resource and to build a following of people with an interest in financial matters.

The best way to build a professional presence on Facebook is by creating a fan page. Fan pages are recognized by the Facebook community as promotional vehicles, and people are willing to follow them as long as they are of interest

37

and provide some value. The advantage of a fan page is that they are visible to any internet user, not just Facebook users, so there is an opportunity to broaden your exposure beyond the community.

Keys to Facebook Success

Build an attractive profile – Your Facebook profile is your magnet for attracting people who would be interested in your thoughts and content. Short of telling people that you are there to promote your business, your profile should include a statement of purpose that lets them know why you are there and how they might benefit from interacting with your page.

Be clear in your intentions. The one thing the Facebook community dislikes the most is phantom promoters. If you stray beyond your stated purpose and cross into an area that begins to resemble a sales pitch, you can quickly alienate your fan base.

Post value: Your posts should contain information, thoughts, ideas, and links that are useful to your fans. One of the easiest ways to post interesting content is to share posts from other users.

Encourage interaction: The whole purpose of residing in the Facebook community is to interact with friends and people with shared interests. The more your page spurs feedback and comments, the more interesting it will appear to the community. Asking thought provoking questions, conducting short surveys, and asking for opinions are effective ways to engage your fans.

Listen actively: The more you engage in active listening, the more interesting people will find you. Look for interesting conversations among your fans and contribute with a comment or a "like." This will get you noticed and people will reciprocate with comments on your page.

LinkedIn

With over 145 million users, LinkedIn doesn't have nearly the reach of Facebook; however, its users are comprised mostly of professionals, business people, and business owners all trying to connect and expand their networks. As connections are made, the opportunity for introductions to other LinkedIn members grows proportionately. Where it used to take years to develop and cultivate a professional network, LinkedIn can shorten the process to a matter of months.

The amazing connective properties of LinkedIn enable anyone to be within six degrees of separation from anyone else. Advisors who understand this can use LinkedIn to get introductions to people with a certain profile who can then introduce them to more influential people, and so on. Advisors can also join groups where people with shared business interests communicate with each other, which is the essence of target marketing.

As with Facebook, shameless self-promoters are discouraged and even ostracized. Networking on LinkedIn is no different than networking at the local business mixer. It's OK to pass along a business card (your LinkedIn profile), and it's acceptable to let people know what you do, but generally, people aren't there to be sold a product or service. They may buy, however, after they have built a relationship, established some trust and benefited from your contributions to the conversation.

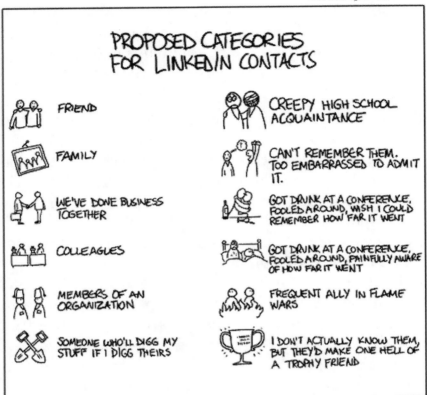

Your Profile is Key

Your LinkedIn profile is the gateway through which others will find and evaluate you. It should be created with your ideal client in mind. Think about the way you would want to be introduced to another professional. The focus should be more on your value proposition and how people benefit by working with you, as opposed to the intricate details of your work history; however, a brief overview your professional credentials and recent experience is essential as well.

Your profile should also include the right keywords that will make it more likely yours will pop up in a Google search. When people search for local professionals, they will use certain keywords in the search box that Google will then match to the most relevant content available for that search. Key words and phrases can be used in your LinkedIn tagline, your title, your profile summary, or in your list of specialties, which makes your profile more searchable.

The use of LinkedIn as a professional networking and business development tool has been expanding rapidly among financial advisors.

Twitter

Twitter is perhaps the most misunderstood of the more popular social media. It often makes the news and late night comedy circuit when attention-starved celebrities use it to boost their tabloid star power. But that's why they use Twitter; because they know that their influence is magnified by the power of Twitter to reach nearly 200 million people. Business people who know how to harness the power of Twitter find it to be the quickest and most effective way to expand their brand and generate traffic.

We've heard stories about financial advisors who have tried incessantly to make contact with high profile and influential people through phone calls and emails, only to be rejected. However, when they reached out to the same people on Twitter, they were welcomed into their network with open arms. From there they simply became part of the conversation and were able to forge a relationship.

NOISE TO SIGNAL
RobCottingham.ca/cartoon

And then, Mr. Bond, once every Twitter user in the world is following me, I'll... I'll... well, I haven't actually thought that far ahead.

It is also interesting that people who spurn cold calls, spam and direct mail, have no problem engaging with brands and business people on Twitter. As with Facebook, the more you listen, and the more you give in the way of value and useful information, the more you will receive in the numbers of followers and in their interaction. The more interesting and useful your tweets are, the more likely they will be retweeted which is how you gain more influence on

Twitter.

Self-promotion is acceptable within limits. You aren't likely to gain any followers or influence if your messages are purely of self-interest, but updates with links to your website, or a recent blog, are fine if they are interspersed among a string of relevant tweets.

For Your Consideration
YouTube

YouTube and other video sharing sites are seeing an explosion of growth as more and more people are gravitating toward video as their preferred means of information gathering. Online video viewing has nearly doubled in the last few years, and the trend show no signs of slowing. Once thought to be the domain of amateur videographers and frustrated entertainers, YouTube has become an essential marketing tool for businesses of all types.

Financial advisors are generating followings by creating and posting informational videos on core financial planning topics. Go to YouTube.com and type in the words "financial planning" to see the number of postings and the number of hits they are getting. Popular formats include interviews with industry experts, simple how-to subject matter, and question-answers on timely topics, or simply posting a webinar. Video postings are an effective way to increase traffic to your website and increase your overall web presence. Your videos can go a long way to building your brand image, so it is important that they are well put together.

Other video sharing & streaming websites we've come across include:

- ✓ www.vimeo.com
- ✓ www.viddler.com

A DAY IN THE LIFE OF AN ADVISOR USING SOCIAL MEDIA

Russ Thornton is a wealth management advisor and Vice President of WealthCare Capital Management. He also spent 12 years as a Financial Consultant with Merrill Lynch. Russ uses social media extensively so we asked him to share with us how he incorporates it into his practice.

Getting the Day Started

7:30 AM – This is usually when I start my day. Despite warnings to the contrary, I'll usually check my email and collect my thoughts on what needs to be accomplished for the day.

8:00 AM – I'll usually login to Hootsuite.com and quickly assess what's going on in the wonderful world of social media. I follow a lot of financial advisors on Twitter, but I also like to keep up with designers, technology thought leaders and some of the vendors whose solutions I use in my business.

8:15 AM – I will check my primary Twitter stream along with a couple of lists I've created. I'm looking for the opportunity to share valuable content and information from others into my followers' stream. And the beauty of Hootsuite is that I can schedule these throughout the day.

Let's say I find 12-15 tweets that I'd like to re-tweet to my followers. I might spread these out over the next 4-5 hours of the day. This allows me to "batch process" some of my social media activities and be more efficient with my time.

8:30 AM – I will check Google Analytics to see what's been happening on my website (www.wealthcarerevolution.com) and see if there's anything unusual that needs to be addressed.

8:45 AM – I will check Squarespace, my blogging platform of choice, to see if there are any blog comments that I need to approve or respond to.

9:00 AM – I typically post 1-2 times per week to my company blog. If I have a post I'd like to publish today, this is typically when I would do it.

In the Office

9:15 AM – Work. Emails. Phone calls. Meetings.

Often, between calls or meetings, I'll take 2-3 minutes to check my Hootsuite account where I can monitor Twitter, Linked In, and Facebook all in one place. This gives me the opportunity to engage in conversations or reply to items where I can add some value.

This is my pattern throughout the typical workday.

Wrap up the Day

4:00 PM – Check Hootsuite again to find opportunities to engage with others. Will batch process items I'd like to share. Confirm that my blog post has been automatically fed into Twitter, LinkedIn, and Facebook. Check my blog.

I usually wrap up my day around 5:30 PM or so. Of course, in the course of any day, my schedule can get thrown into a tailspin and it's all I can do to keep my head above water, but in the rare event of a relatively calm day, this gives you an idea of my schedule.

As a financial advisor, I have some other considerations to make while engaging in social media like Twitter. Primary among them . . .

Compliance

So, what do I do to make sure I'm taking all the necessary precautions and steps to ensure that I don't run afoul of the regulators? Well the first thing I do is think before I type. Common sense will go a long way in helping you avoid problems.

However, my secret compliance weapon in using social media is Arkovi (www.arkovi.com). Arkovi has created an archiving solution that works in the background. It's unobtrusive and doesn't alter the way I interact with the tools I choose to utilize. Currently, I use Arkovi to back up all of social media sites including Twitter, Facebook, LinkedIn, YouTube as well as a my blog. And if a new social media platform pops up tomorrow, as long as it has an RSS feed, Arkovi can back it up.

Meetup

If you prefer the more traditional method of networking, the easiest way to connect with groups of like-minded people in your community is through Meetup.com (www.meetup.com). It combines the people-finding technology of the web with all the advantages of face-to-face networking.

Essentially, Meetup is a web directory of clubs, organizations and community groups that have organized for the purpose of bringing like-minded people together physically to network, learn and share business and social activities. Presently, there are over 37,000 Meetup groups that meet nearly 80,000 times a month on 3,500 topics in over 4,000 cities.

Anyone can start a Meetup group and post it on the user board. With over 4 million users looking to join groups of shared interests, it's possible to put yourself in front of a few dozen people with just a few clicks of the mouse. It's best to first join other groups so that you can build a network of friends and establish your expertise. You may find that groups that meet on topics or activities completely unrelated to your field, such as social or fitness groups, can be the best source of prospects.

Look Out For Yourself: Monitoring Your Reputation

Becoming active in social media circles has proven to be a sure path to increased visibility, stature and brand awareness. At the same time, it can be the quickest way to tarnishing your reputation especially if you are unaware of how your web presence is being perceived by your followers. All it takes is one comment or post from a trasher to start the process. Fortunately, there are tools available that enable you to monitor your brand and protect your reputation. The following are the top three free tools you can use to monitor your name and brand with just a few clicks:

Tweet Deck (www.tweetdeck.com) is a social media dashboard that enables you to track updates and posts of all the main networking sites such as Twitter, Facebook and LinkedIn. You can organize the dashboard by columns for each site, and you can set up keyword searches that will retrieve any updates that include your name.

Social Mention (www.socialmention.com) combs all of the major social media sites for user created content (posts, updates and tweets) based on search terms you give it. You will receive an email update with a complete list of mentions of your name or any topic you put in your search terms.

Google Alerts (www.google.com/alerts) operates in much the same way as Social Mention, except it tracks content all over the web. You will receive email updates that include any article, blog post and tweet that includes your name.

Summary

The social media revolution is here, and it has transformed our society unlike any previous communications technology. You can decide not to join the conversation; however, if you want to be visible to your markets, you need put yourself among them–where they congregate, communicate and connect with other people. And for a growing segment of the wired-in population, that is in cyber communities such as Facebook, LinkedIn and Twitter.

A social media strategy should be a cornerstone of an effective overall web marketing strategy. On its own, social media can be a boon to a small business that needs to forge a reputation and build brand awareness. When used in the context of a complete web strategy, social media becomes the engine that drives interested visitor traffic to your branded website where they are more likely to convert themselves into a qualified prospect.

CHAPTER EXERCISE

✓ Contact you Compliance department to get any guidelines about the various social media sites. Are there any that you can or can not use? What type of archiving tool do you need to consider?

✓ If you have not already done so, sign up for accounts with the social media websites of your choice and complete your basic profiles.

✓ For an excellent read on how social media is revolutionizing business, we recommend the book, Sociable! How Social Media is Turning Sales and Marketing Upside-down, by Shane Gibson and Stephen Jagger.

✓ For more ideas on how to use social media in your practice, visit our blog at www.advisorwebsites.com/blog

4 NEWSLETTER/EMAIL MARKETING

"Diamonds are forever. E-mail comes close."

- June Kronholz

It seems like so long ago when the only real communication we had through the internet was with email. There was a time, in fact, when we would look forward to opening our email inbox because we sort of knew what to expect. These days, we almost cringe as we click the inbox button because we know that we will find an overwhelming clutter of spam and distractions. If that is the new "normal" for email communication, you would think that the days of effective email marketing are over, especially with the meteoric rise of social media and instant messaging.

Think again. According to most marketing researchers, email marketing is still among the top two marketing methods for generating maximum ROI. Done right, an email-newsletter marketing campaign can have the greatest overall impact on your visibility, your web presence and, ultimately, your bottom line.

Why Financial Advisors Use It

Five biggest reasons that financial advisors cite for implementing a newsletter-email marketing campaign[12]:

---

12 http://www.advisorwebsites.com/blog/marketing/10-e-mail-marketing-tips-for-financial-advisors/

1. It's inexpensive, easy to use and quick. Responses to your email newsletter can come within minutes of its distribution.
2. It's an effective way of touching your clients and prospects to build relationships and trust.
3. It enables you to target your markets by segmenting your list.
4. It's data driven so you can easily measure ROI and overall effectiveness.
5. It provides a value-added service that your clients appreciate.

Why It Works

You Have Their Permission

The key distinction of newsletter email marketing is that it is permission-based in that you are actually invited by your clients and prospects to market to them. With that comes a responsibility on your part not to abuse that permission and to ensure that your communications continue to meet their needs. Just as quickly as you are invited, you can become uninvited.

It's a Proper Way to Court

All experts in marketing to the affluent will tell you that high net worth people need to be courted before they will even consider a professional relationship with you. The courting process can take as many as 25 contacts consisting of phone calls, follow-up emails, letters, and meetings. Newsletter emails count among those contacts, and are a high-value and low-intrusive way to cultivate the relationship.

They Get What They Want

Your clients and prospects are always looking for information that can help them. Newsletter emails will be welcomed by your clients and prospects as long as they meet their specific needs. By segmenting your list, you can provide more targeted information based on demographics, interests and even occupational specialty. This requires that you know your target markets and the type of information they want.

How to Launch a Successful Email Marketing Campaign

Start with a great list. Your best list is your client list, and you may also have a list of prospects who are well-cultivated. These are people you know and who will likely grant you permission to add them to your newsletter list.

Always be collecting email addresses. List building for financial advisors needs to be done organically and incrementally. Every person who becomes a prospect should be invited to join your list. In the course of your regular business networking, at social functions, networking meetings, trade shows, and through your website, you should promote your newsletter and ask permission to include them on your newsletter list.

Set expectations. Let your list know what they can expect from you in the form of email communications. If it is a newsletter, let them know how often it will be distributed and the kind of information they can expect to receive, and then deliver on those expectations.

Deliver quality and value. Your email communications, especially your newsletter should reflect the professional image you want to convey. The information should be timely, relevant, and offer something of value. It is highly recommended that you partner with a financial newsletter provider known for quality content and production.

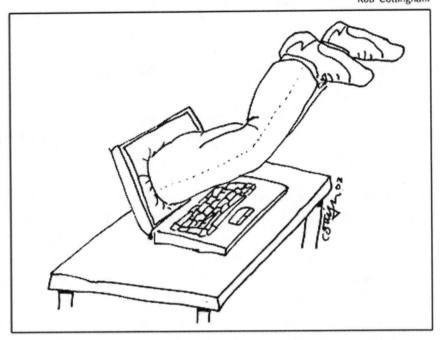

NOISE TO SIGNAL
Rob Cottingham

Chris Turgeson, 1974-2007. Clicked send, instantly regretted it, tried to retrieve the email. He will be missed.

Segment your list. It is important to keep their attention. If you send out information on college savings to your high net-worth empty nester clients, you will lose their attention and possibly send a message that you don't understand their needs. Segment your lists so that you can direct targeted information to each of your market segments.

Phone follow-up is key. It is important to combine marketing tactics in order to boost overall results. You should follow up newsletter emails every couple of months with a phone call. Use these opportunities to find out what they like about the newsletter, what they'd like to see, and, of course, if any particular article struck a chord with them.

Close the marketing loop. Make sure your newsletter and email communications include links to your website, blog and social media sites. Remember, one of the overall goals of a complete internet marketing strategy is to increase your visibility and enhance your brand.

Monitor results. The advantage of most web-based marketing tools is their measurability. With electronic newsletters you can measure many aspects of your viewership that will tell you how well your newsletters are received.

More on List Building

The key to list building is to make it easy for people to subscribe to your newsletter. You can provide easy access from all of your web portals such as your website and your social media sites, as well as your email signature. When people opt-in or subscribe on their own, they have given you their permission to market to them.

Here are some quick tips on maximizing access to your newsletter:

Add an opt-in subscription box or a link to one or all of your websites including your social media sites such as Facebook and LinkedIn. On your own website, include an opt-in box in several locations such as the landing page, your biography page and on your comments page.

Announce updates. Whenever you publish a newsletter, announce it on your social media sites by posting an update. You can tweet about it on Twitter and include an excerpt from your newsletter on Facebook.

Simplify the process. Keep the opt-in process short and simple. All you need initially is their email address and a name. You'll have other opportunities to gather more information later.

Use an auto-responder. You need an automated system to gather and process the subscriptions. A good auto-responder system will also help you organize and segment your contacts, create campaigns, and analyze your data. If your newsletter service doesn't offer this, you should consider using a software solution such as Constant Contact, MailChimp, or AWeber.

Summary

In spite of all that is objectionable about emailing today, it still remains the preferred mode of communication for busy, successful people. While most people are drowning in the noise of constant messaging from all forms of media, they will still open an email when they are expecting it. Financial advisors who understand the rules of engagement for permission-based email marketing are realizing huge returns on their investment.

CHAPTER EXERCISE

✓ Review any newsletters you subscribe to. Why do you find them valuable? How often do you receive them? What kind of newsletter content would be valuable to your clients?

✓ Research some reputable email marketing software services. Maybe your head office already has this set up for you. Decide which solution would work well for you. (We personally use www.mailchimp.com)

✓ If you have not already done so, add a newsletter sign up box to your website.

5 TO BLOG OR NOT TO BLOG

"A blogger is constantly looking over his shoulder, for fear that he is not being followed."

- Robert Brault

Would it surprise you to know that a growing number of Americans now look to microblogs as their primary source of advice and solutions?[13] In recent years bloggers have become the new influencers on the web. Internet usage studies show that blogs have become a magnet for people looking for their daily dose of news and commentaries, and they now turn to blogs for remedies for all of life's ailments, including their financial planning needs.

For much of the last decade, blogging was primarily the domain of individuals, generally people who used the new blogosphere to air their views, share their hobbies, and promote their causes—and many of them found a way to make a buck. Just in the last few years the vibrant and casual nature of blogs has become an essential communication outlet for businesses, providing them with a way to reach

---

13 *"As social media outlets continue to surface and we allow our connections to the world to grow, the very definition of the word social will continue to evolve. Sites such as Twitter and Facebook will become more important to us… we will turn there first when needing advice and opinions, when wanting to find out what is happening in the world and when hoping to gain other perspectives. It doesn't matter if we are looking for breaking news stories or the hottest new disco club in the city. Social media is where we will figure out the answers."* Chris Pirillo, Social Media Expert. http://Chris.Pirillo.com

out to their market on familiar terms. The biggest boon to businesses has been the opening of a two-way communication with their markets that is the nature of blogging.

Today, more businesses than ever are pointing to blogging as their most important inbound marketing initiative. And the vast majority of businesses report that their blogs have led to increased visibility, notoriety, and business development. Financial advisors are finding that blogging is an affordable way to establish themselves as a high-profile authority and a credible source of financial information in a highly competitive arena.

What Exactly is a Blog?

A blog is much like a digital journal, a self-publishing device on a website that enables you to share your thoughts, ideas and insights on a nearly unlimited scale. It is very much like a newsletter that you distribute to your client and prospects; only, with a blog, there is the potential to reach far beyond your CRM database to thousands of people who are looking for financial advice.

Operating in digital space, a well-structured blog is a cyber-marketing platform that can expand your capacity to cultivate relationships, attract new clients, build trust and credibility, enhance your reputation, and expand your influence.

The popularity of blogs can be traced to the fact that they enable the reader to interact with the blogger through a "comments" section. From a business perspective, this is invaluable because it enables the business to interact with its market, gain valuable feedback, collect data, and build a loyal following of like-minded people. Isn't that what marketing is all about? Now it can be done with a simple blog post.

Why You Need a Blog AND a Website

Remember that your website is the central hub for your web marketing strategy. It is a more formal structure that guides your visitors through the complete story that you want to tell about your services. It is where your product and service information is housed. It is a source of educational materials and resource tools for your clients. It is your primary branding platform where your target market goes to learn about you and your values and philosophy. It is also your source of data and information about your visitors that can help you direct your sales and marketing efforts.

A blog is a less formal communication tool that allows you to peel the layers off of your persona as you speak directly to your target market. People still like to do business with real people, so they want to get to know the person behind the website. An effective blog, with regular posts that reflect the thoughts and insights of the blogger, can do much more to create a bond with the reader than a static website by itself.

But there is a true marketing purpose for a blog, and that is to drive traffic to your website where the call to action can take place. When done correctly, with the use of keywords that catch the attention of the search engines, an active blog can attract many more visitors than a static website. Readers who find the blog posts to be interesting enough may be enticed to click the link that will take them directly to your website.

A recent study by HubSpot found that small companies with a blog get 55% more traffic to their website. They also get 97% more inbound links and 434% more indexed pages, which means your site will have more authority with search engines and is more likely to be found[14]. So, blogging is as much about driving potential business to your website as it is to differentiate you as an online authority.

14 Hubspot.com Blog Aug 19,2009 Study Shows Small Businesses That Blog Get 55% More Website Visitors http://blog.hubspot.com/blog/tab-id/6307/bid/5014/Study-Shows-Small-Businesses-That-Blog-Get-55-More-Web-site-Visitors.aspx

Hi! My name's Kelly, and I'll be blogging about this later tonight.

If You Build it (a Blog), They Will Come

If you have ever used a newsletter in your marketing efforts, you know that, in addition to finding or creating the content, you need to build your own list of recipients. This is done slowly and incrementally over time by soliciting email addresses. When you create a blog and communicate through the internet, people will find you and invite themselves to join in your conversation. Not only that, if the information is worth sharing, they'll invite others to join, so your list growth will be self-propelled.

There are two key elements in blogging that are responsible for this phenomenon: **search engines** and **social media engagement**.

1.) **Search Engines will find you**. For every blog post that you publish, search engines will find a new page and a new set of keywords contained in your title, body copy, and corresponding tags. Basically, having a blog increases your keyword rankings, which makes it easier for search engines to find your site.

These search engines, like Google, use bots to crawl the web and index web sites. If they find new content, the bot comes back more often. As with keywords, search engines like sites with fresh content, and having a blog is an easy way to ensure that your content is regularly updated. You may not even know you're doing it, but having a blog has helped optimize your site and grow your organic search traffic.

2.) **Blogs are social engagement mechanisms** that make it exceedingly easy for people to share your posts with others. For example, when a client reads your post and then wants to share it with some friends, it's only a matter of a couple of mouse clicks to have a link to your blog posted on his or her Facebook page. Your blog can be equipped with an automatic social media publisher that will instantly send your post link to all of your social media sites, such as Twitter, LinkedIn, and Facebook, once you publish it, which will start the sharing process among your networks. You'll see traffic to your blog increase quickly and steadily.

There is divided opinion on whether your blog should reside on its own website or as part of your main website. As a separate website, your blog could work to provide additional external back links to your main website which helps to raise its ranks in the search engines. The downside is that you will have two websites to maintain.

10 TIPS TO ENSURE HIGH TRAFFIC TO YOUR BLOG SITE:

1. **Host your blog on your domain**. If it is set up as a sub-domain with an internal link to your website, it makes it easier for search engines to find, and it will be indexed separately from your website, which can improve your search results.

2. **Use images, graphs and charts** to help convey your message and improve readability.

3. **Encourage sharing and comments**. The more external links you can create to your site the higher it will rank in the search engines.

4. **Optimize your blog title and content**. Using some basic Search Engine Optimization techniques will greatly improve your blog's visibility.

5. **Make sure your message is targeted**. Know your audience. If you are writing about what they want to know about, they will find you.

6. **Promote your site wherever and whenever you can**. Make sure your URL is attached to your business card, your email signature and all of your social media sites.

7. **Update your blog frequently**. The more updates, the more often the search engines will find and rank you. We recommend publishing a new blog post at least monthly.

8. **Have your blog updates posted to your social media sites** such as Twitter, Facebook and LinkedIn.

9. **Become a guest blogger on high traffic blogs**. If you can find an opportunity to post a guest blog on another well visited site, it can raise both your notoriety and traffic to your own blog.

10. **Post comments on popular blogs or in forums**. This can increase your visibility, and you will be creating more back links to your own site.

One approach we sometimes recommend is that your blog reside on your main website as it will be much easier to maintain it, and from an SEO perspective, it will generate fresh, new content for your website which is just as important as back links. Plus, you can create internal links between your main website pages and your blog.

Aren't Blogs a Compliance Nightmare?

Generally, financial advisors have been slow to adapt to the blogosphere due largely to industry regulations and compliance issues. This is rapidly changing as more compliance departments are establishing guidelines for blogging and introducing mechanisms for getting them approved more quickly. The good news is that a blog is one of the easiest forms of online content to manage for compliance purposes.

If you are living in the US, all blog content, including comments, is considered static content and needs to be pre-approved before being published. If you are an SEC registered advisor or a state regulated investment advisor, you will first need to write the content and then wait for the compliance department to review and approve it before you can publish it to your blog.

If you are an advisor affiliated with a broker dealer, the process is similar. The only difference is that the content may also have to be submitted to FINRA, and the wait time for approval will be slightly longer as it is not handled internally. While the content must be archived for a minimum of three years, Arkovi recommends six years, and with their solution, you can easily archive your blog content and comments by using the RSS feed that is contained in 99% of blogs.

Is Blogging Right For You?

Truth be told, blogging is not for everyone. To do it right, it can takes a commitment of time and discipline. Unless you are able to update your blog at least once a month, it may not have the kind of impact that would make it worth your while. Although much of the work in setting up and maintaining a blog can be outsourced or delegated to a staff person, it is another important facet of your brand that needs to be managed.

If, however, you do like the idea of becoming a thought leader by differentiating yourself from the rest, and you have a couple of hours a month to devote to writing, blogging can be the most effective marketing activity you can perform, with an unparalleled return on your investment. If it is important for you to increase your visibility in the industry and elevate your stature and credibility among your target market, then you should not overlook blogging as a way to grow your web presence.

CHAPTER EXERCISE

✓ Review 2 or 3 financial industry related blogs to get an idea of the types of posts that would be useful to your clients and prospects.

✓ Write 1 or 2 sample blog posts you could envision using on you blog. Did you like writing them? Could you commit to a regular posting schedule? If not, could you consider hiring a professional copy writer to help you out?

✓ If you move forward with blogging, consider enabling social media sharing.

6　ON THE WEB, CONTENT IS KING

"Getting information off the internet is like taking a drink from a fire hydrant."

- Mitchell Kapor

Crown Your Website with Good Content

In the wonderful World Wide Web content is king. It's the primary reason people go online–to be informed, to find answers, to solve problems. Frankly, many internet users want to be astounded. The ease with which internet surfers can click out of one site and onto the next renders any content-poor site into a fleeting flash of colors, buried for good in the history archive. Time is money for your online clients and prospects, and they are looking for value in return for their time.

Websites that contain a variety of categories that are updated periodically with quality, fresh, content will grab more attention than those that are nothing more than a single page electronic brochure. Relevant, compelling content is the key to attracting new visitors to your site, keeping them there, and keeping them coming back. It is also the way to grab the attention of the search engines and ensure that your site climbs in the ranks. But, for content to have this effect, it must be constantly updated so it continues to be relevant and timely.

Content for a Financial Advisor's website

In Chapter 2, we outlined some of the content pieces that financial advisors might want to include on their websites. While this is a matter of preference, your website is your introduction to the world, so it should contain essential information that you want your market to know about you and your practice. Below are popular content components that add vital information in the form of static content to your site:

- ✓ Personal bio
- ✓ Company bio
- ✓ Products and services
- ✓ Useful Resources
- ✓ Social media profiles
- ✓ Community involvement
- ✓ Testimonials (Canada Only)

Static content is essential because it provides the foundational information about you and your practice. Once up on your website, it will require minimal updating. You may want to add content updates to your website in order to make your site more visible to the search engines and more engaging for your clients and other visitors. Types of content updates may include:

- ✓ A blog (see Chapter 5)
- ✓ Timely articles of interest
- ✓ News updates
- ✓ Event announcements

How to Create Great Web Content

Web readers want web content, not print content

People consume content on the web much differently than they do from print. Consider the way you read web content.

Chances are you skim and scan. If you're not engaged by the first paragraph, you move on. You scroll through the headlines or subheadings. And, if the article seems to ramble on (past a few hundred words), you look for something shorter to read.

If that's you, you're not alone. Seventy-nine percent of internet users scan web pages instead of reading word-for-word, and because people read 25% more slowly from a computer screen, they become restless.[15]

Knowing that people read differently online, it becomes vitally important to structure your web content differently than you would for a magazine or printed newsletter. The look, feel, and structure of your content become critical elements.

Your content needs to be both visually engaging and easy to consume. Online readers don't want to wait for the last paragraph to get the key points they're looking for; and they want their content in small bites, not huge mouthfuls that are difficult to swallow.

---

15   Jakob Nielsen, "How Users Read on the Web" (Web. Oct 1997)

TEN QUICK TIPS TO HELP YOU WRITE GOOD WEB CONTENT

✓ **Let your ideas flow** – The best way to get your thoughts down on paper is to let them flow freely. Don't worry about content, style, grammar or structure, yet. Edit later, or outsource your draft/outline to an editor or ghostwriter.

✓ **Punch your key ideas** – Each paragraph should contain one main idea – use a second paragraph for a second idea, since users tend to skip any second point as they scan over the paragraph. Design your web document to be scanable.

✓ **Write upside down** – Use an inverted pyramid style of writing. Users don't like to scroll through masses of text, so put the most important information at the top.

✓ **Less is more** – make the word count for the online version of a given topic about half the word count used when writing for print. Users find it painful to read too much text on screens, and they read about 25 percent more slowly from screens than from paper.

✓ **KISS your writing** – Convoluted writing and complex words are even harder to understand online. Limit your paragraphs to two to four sentences and the length of your articles to less than 600 words.

✓ **Be conversational** – Online readers expect a less formal style of writing. A conversational tone is more engaging, and it allows your personality to show through.

✓ **Use images** – Images and photos draw the eye and make your content more visually engaging. Be sure your images are credited properly.

✓ **Use bulleted and numbered lists** – lists slow down the scanning eye and can draw attention to important points.

✓ **Avoid clever headings** – do not use cute headings since users rely on scanning to pick up the meaning of the text.

✓ **Keep an idea journal** – Great ideas for new content can be fleeting so it's important to have a place on your computer, your smart phone, or a stack of post-it notes to record ideas as they come to you. Ideas can also come from articles, blogs and commentaries that you read every day online, so set up a folder in your browser to hold bookmarked sites.

How to Write an Effective Biography for your Financial Website

A winning biography will give clients and prospects information about you that helps them to determine if you are a good match for their needs and will allow them to have an idea about your strengths and achievements. A good bio should always tell the following in an engaging way:

✓ who you are
✓ your area of expertise
✓ your unique value proposition

Your bio is your personal promotion and an opportunity to make a connection with your website visitors. It provides details that reveal your personality, so people can get a sense of what working with you will be like.

Although website bios are not limited by page length, it is a good idea to be selective about the details you include. Online readers tend to skim through content and we recommend that you format your bio with bullets, short paragraphs and bold important information.

The following list of details can help you construct a comprehensive bio. Feel free to respond to as many questions as you consider relevant, and include additional details that are important to you.

1. Your professional details
✓ Financial title i.e., *Investment Representative, Financial Planner etc.*
✓ Number of years in the industry. Instead of stating the number of years, which cannot be kept current, list the year in which you started in the business.
✓ Have you had more than one role in the financial industry? Describe and give the number of years in each role i.e., *Financial Advisor, Associate, Management Experience, etc.*

- ✓ Do you have other relevant experience? Describe and indicate how this relates to the work you do today and how it can enhance your ability to help clients.
- ✓ Why should clients choose you as their financial advisor?
- ✓ What do you most enjoy about helping clients?
- ✓ How do you keep in touch with clients and provide them with the information they need?

2. Your qualifications
- ✓ Education
- ✓ Published works
- ✓ Awards and professional distinctions i.e., *Rookie advisor award etc.*
- ✓ Professional designation i.e., *CFP, CLU etc.*

3. Your values and beliefs
- ✓ What is your value proposition?
- ✓ What makes you unique and how will your clients benefit from that?
- ✓ What are your strengths?
- ✓ What are your beliefs about the profession?
- ✓ Do you work with a special market(s) i.e., *retirees, ethnic market, families, business owners, etc.*
- ✓ How can you help these markets?

4. Your community involvement
- ✓ Describe your community involvement and explain why it is important to you

5. Your personal details
- ✓ Marital and family status (if you wish)
- ✓ Hobbies and interest (can be really effective if you target a special market group or can sometimes provide a

great source of conversation during your initial meeting with some prospects)

It is acceptable to start your bio with first person references and, midway, change to the third person. Try to incorporate your own personal style and make your copy engaging. This will allow you to sell yourself through your bio and reach out to most of your readers.

Below is an example of a biography covering most of the aspects discussed above:

SAMPLE BIOGRAPHY

"John Doe has been with the Financial Company Group since 2006. He believes his previous five years as a sales manager selling health products to the medical industry were an ideal foundation for his work as a financial advisor.

Attention to detail, good listening skills and great empathy are symbols of his appreciation by his clients. He is effectively supported by a team of administration, group benefits and investment products specialists whose teamwork and professionalism help him build long-term relationships with his growing client base and provide excellent customer service.

John is a proud recipient of University XYZ's MBA of Finance and was recently invited to join the Million Dollar Round Table. His focus is on doctors and health practitioners.

John is happily married to his lovely wife, Jane, and he has two lovely daughters. Away from the business, he enjoys golfing, skiing and spending time with his family and friends."

For electronic versions of this and additional templates and samples that may be most applicable for your practice visit our blog at www.advisorwebsites.com/blog .

Make Your Content Compelling

Adding compelling content is essential in order to create a successful website, but if you're going to expend any amount of time or resources in doing so, it is important to ensure that it adds value to your visitors' experience. You don't necessarily have to astound them, but you do need to try to engage them and produce an experience that they will want to repeat and possibly share with others. The best way to do this is by adding external content and tools that are relevant and useful to your target market.

Successful advisor websites are resource-rich with externally created tools and content that increase the chances that visitors will bookmark the site for future reference. They may include financial calculators, stock tickers, financial forms, client portals and log ins, or financial news aggregates, such as Yahoo Finance, along with guest bloggers, newsletters, or daily commentaries.

Using external content can be an easy and economical way to add a dynamic edge to your website; however, there are some key points to consider when selecting it:

1. Will the content be **of value to your visitors**? Internet users are always looking for new information presented in different ways. They want to be educated and they want to be able to interact with the resources.
2. Is the material **copyrighted**? If you use any videos, pictures, or graphics be sure to check the copyrights and any terms of use.
3. Do you require **3rd party approval** from the content owner? Some materials may not require approval from

content providers, but it is good practice to inform them of your intent to use their material.

4. Do you require approval from your **compliance** department? Most compliance departments require that all external materials be submitted for approval. Some Broker Dealers have a library of approved tools and content that can be freely added.

5. Will the content **change** over time? It is important that your site's content not become outdated. Articles and blogs can be archived by date, but other materials, such as financial forms or calculators, may need updating. Sometimes it is more manageable to link directly to the resource rather than to try maintaining it on your site. Some tools, such as stock tickers and news aggregators, stream updates directly to your site.

Once you've answered these five questions you can start exploring different types of external content. Don't worry about finding everything you think you'll need right away. Content can be added at anytime, and sometimes it is best to add content incrementally as this keeps the search engines coming back to your site. When you find some content to add, you simply add it yourself if you are using a user friendly platform or contact your website provider, and they can have it up on your site that same day.

NOISE TO SIGNAL
Rob Cottingham · socialsignal.com/n2s

Sure, I've made some bad choices. Doing that "Name 25 illegal things you've done recently" blog meme is probably at the top of my list.

Dynamic Content

Content that is updated real time or through visitor requests not only makes your website more vibrant, it can increase your traffic flow and stickiness. Adding RSS feeds of streaming financial news, stock tickers, Twitter feeds, are all ways to keep you content dynamic, and incorporating applicable resources, such as calculators and other way to interact with your clients increases the amount of time your visitors will spend on your website.

The more successful advisor websites include a client portal through which communications can flow in both directions. With their highly secured encryption technology, the communications through dedicated client portals can be more secure than email, especially when attaching documents. The more important reason for adopting resources such as client communication portals is that it elevates your relationships with your clients and ensures constant and near instant contact. With these types of resources, your website can become more essential and collaborative for your clients.

For example, CRM Software, a leading office management and client relationship management system, has made the reporting and client communications functions of its popular CRM and portfolio aggregation system, Junxure, (www.junxure.com) available to financial advisors and their clients through a client portal application called ClientView Live. In addition to delivering on-demand reports to clients, it opens up a two-way online workflow communication between advisors and clients. Its secure document vault enables both client and advisor to store and access critical financial documents that can be used individually or collaboratively.

Content Sources

Many advisors have neither the time nor inclination to create web content or write articles for their web presence, all of which can be outsourced for a reasonable cost. This approach can save a tremendous amount of time and effort.

For example, providers like McGraw-Hill Financial Communications (www.visitfc.com) offer a variety of products ranging from content packages for your website, newsletters, calculators and social media communications including FINRA-reviewed articles and pre-written posts usable in your social media sites.

But, for those advisors who want to differentiate themselves as authorities or experts, and who want to use their sites to build rapport with their target market, writing content, such as a weekly blog, or a timely article, can be extremely rewarding.

Content sources abound and you may want to use a combination of them to keep your site lively and diverse in its offerings. These are some of the ways financial advisors add useful and relevant content to their sites:

Source	Pros	Cons
Create it yourself	No monetary cost; original work that establishes your authority	Time intensive; requires good writing skills; compliance delays
Partner with professional writers or communication firms	High, consistent quality; tailored to your style/message	Cost
Purchase from content provider	Access to large archive of articles, newsletters;	Content may be too generic; low search engine ranking
Leverage existing relationships, i.e. broker dealer, website provider	Access; compliance ready; low or no cost	Generic quality

Combination of sources	Utilize strengths of various sources, i.e., one might be better at creating a bio, another is a better source for articles; can control monetary and time costs	None, except as they apply to each source listed above

Summary

When you go to the web, whether as a reader or a provider, it's all about the content. The difference between a good website that is well visited and one that simply becomes a placeholder on the web is the quality, usefulness and relevance of the content. For financial advisors who are serious about employing a web marketing strategy to differentiate them and expand their visibility, attention to the type and quality of their web content is paramount. Creating or finding compelling content does not have to be time or money consuming; however, in website marketing, there is an almost direct correlation between quality and return on investment.

CHAPTER EXERCISE

✓ Review your personal / company bio. Is it up to date? Does it need revisions? If so, this is the perfect time.

✓ Do a Google search for your company / practice using keywords you think your clients and prospects would be using. Are you getting the results you are expecting? If not consider re-writing some of your content.

7 MARKETING YOUR WEBSITE

"Never let your ads write checks that your website can't cash."

- Avinash Kaushik

This book has been devoted to getting your pump primed for launching a successful internet marketing strategy. Once it is in place, all of the key components covered in the previous chapters –your branded website, your blog, your social media sites, and your e-newsletter– are wired together to create an interconnected web of activity that will continue to gain momentum over time.

The magic of an effective web strategy is that, with a solid launch, your results will climb over time while your investment of time and resources declines. The key is to optimize your strategy early by utilizing proven web marketing techniques. This chapter provides an overview of core marketing techniques that can be applied even as you are in the process of getting the pieces of your strategy in place. While it is not an exhaustive list, it covers the most widely used methods for increasing your web presence and maximizing your marketing efforts.

Web Promotion Basics

Promoting a website has become an accepted societal and business norm, in fact, it has become an expectation. "Go to my website at www...." has nearly replaced "here's my business card" in many business settings. In fact, for the wired-in, tech-savvy public, websites are the new calling card. So, promote away. You can be a little shameless - say it, write it, print it, repeat it, and include it in just about any personal or digital interaction you have with the public.

Here are a few simple, but very effective ways to promote your website:

Business Card. Did we really need to mention this one? Don't wait until you use up those brand new boxes of business cards you just bought. Get some new ones made ASAP with your URL address on the front <u>and</u> the back. The same goes for your letterhead and other literature where your contact information is included. You can also add your social media profile links for Twitter, Facebook, LinkedIn and other social media sites.

Email Signature. Most email providers enable you to automatically add a signature to your email which can include your website URL address and social media profile links. Include a call to action in a larger or slightly different font. Something along the lines of *"Check out my brand new website at www.yourwebsite.com!"* or *"Sign up for my quarterly newsletter on my website at www.yourwebsite.com"* can work well.

Social Media Sites. Add your URL address to each of your Facebook, Twitter and LinkedIn profiles. Make sure you optimize your link title/anchor text. (i.e. instead of having "website" as the inline text to your company website, consider using "Company Name" or "Keyword A" where keyword links to your website)

Voice Mail. This is one you may not have thought of. It is common practice to include a web address in a recorded voice mail message. You can simply add "…and please visit my website at www…" at the end of your message.

Client and Prospect Contact. Don't be afraid to alert your clients and prospects to the fact they have a new resource and a new way to communicate with you. Put a post-it note near your phone to remind you to mention your website at the end of every conversation. Simple as, "By the way, I just launched my new website and I think you'll find it to be of value. I'd be especially interested in your thoughts on the _____ section. Please let me know what you think."

Traffic Building Essentials

The success of a commercial website is dependent upon the same principal success factor of a brick-and-mortar business – location, location, location. If you own a sandwich shop, you want your shop to be located where nearby traffic will find it. The same goes for your website, except the nearby traffic are the millions of people jamming the search highway looking for shortcuts to their information needs. In order for the traffic to find you, your web property needs to be located where the traffic can find you easily, on the first couple of pages of the search engines.

In Chapter 2, we provided you with some key elements for optimizing your website. Even a fully optimized website will lose some of its lustre with the search engines unless there are some additional ways for them to find and rank it. Essentially, your website needs some juice to keep the search engine bots coming back.

Get Quality Links to Your Site. One way to get some juice to your website is by getting inbound links. Inbound links are one of the most influential factors in search engine results and high rankings. This is particularly true when these links come from trusted and established websites. These are usually referred to as authoritative domains, and Google or Yahoo will rank your pages really high if these domains link to your website.

Social Media Links. One of the primary objectives of your social media strategy is to build brand awareness and authority by connecting with your clients and target market where they like to meet. Another very critical objective of maintaining an active social media presence is to create more linkage back to your main website. Each time you post an update that references a new blog post or article, it creates another back link to your site. Then, each time your post is shared or retweeted, additional back links are created. You can achieve the same effect by becoming active on forums and blogs by leaving comments which will also create back links.

Start a Blog. We covered blogging in Chapter 5 where we stressed their value as a way to build your presence and authority. It also is a way to add fresh content to your website so that the search engine bots come around more often. Each blog post will create an internal link to your main website, which can also improve your site's rankings.

Write Articles for Others to Use in Websites and Newsletters. You can raise your visibility by spreading your wings as an expert. Website and e-newsletter editors are always looking for fresh, informative content, so be generous with yours and get your articles published on other sites. Your articles should include an author's profile with your website's URL in it. Your article has the potential to go "viral" if additional website editors decide to publish it as well. This could generate a lot of back links to your main website. You can achieve the same effect by submitting your approved articles to article directories such as EzineArticles.com.

Social Bookmarking: By creating engaging and compelling content, your visitors are more likely to feel it could be of value to others. Social media sites such as Digg, De.licio.us, Reddit, and Stumbleupon allow your audience to bookmark your pages, share them among their friends, or submit excerpts to aggregator sites. These websites will syndicate your content and make it available to a massive pool of readers. In doing so, back links to your website are automatically created which will increase its visibility to the search engines. You can encourage your visits to bookmark your site by adding a widget to your page that enables them to add your site with the click of a mouse.

**Inbound links are down slightly against trackbacks,
while comments edged up against Diggs in late-day trading.**

Pay Per Click (PPC) Advertising

When you do a search on search engines, you are presented
with at least two different kinds of results: the first are actual
webpage results from organic listings, and the second one
are paid or sponsored listings. You can usually find the paid
listings at the top of the search results and on the side bars.
On the illustration below, I searched for '*iPhone*' on Google
and highlighted the paid listings in the two sections.

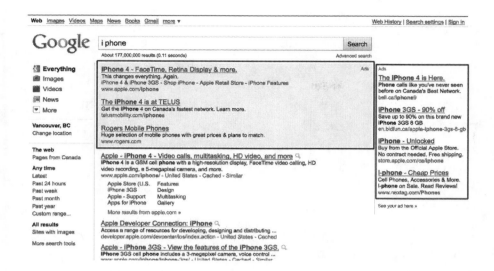

The latest statistics show that 70% of search engines users click on the organic results, while only 30% click on the pay per click ads. However, 95% of users won't go beyond the first page of search results[16]. That's where pay per click (PPC) comes into play.

The goal of sponsored listings is to have your website presented on the first page of the search engines like Google, Yahoo! or Bing. The beauty of search engine marketing is that you are targeting users at the precise moment THEY are looking for you, your products or services.

How does it work?

Think about this as an auction for keywords. Going back to my example with the iPhone there could be seven or eight ads listed on the right side of the Google search results. Every time someone clicks on the bottom ad, the company running the ad pays Google 50 cents per click. The company above them might be paying 75 cents per click. Basically, they are

---

16   iProspect Search Engine User Behavior Study (April 2006)

bidding to get toward the top (the ad costs given are not actual costs, they are only here to support the explanation).

Pay per click advertising is a combination of a science and an art. The science part is that you can, with some certainty, imagine the keywords that will produce the clicks. The artistic part is related to the ad piece that you need to write, making sure it is compelling enough for your target audience to click on your sponsored listing.

Why it works

The reason why billions of dollars are flowing from traditional advertising to online advertising is simply because you have the ability to know with certainty which ad works and which doesn't, and you know that if you spend X, you'll get Y. Pay per click gives you control over your advertising; it is efficient, and basically, you can calculate your ROI down to the penny.

Do's and don'ts

The important part to remember is that the competition can be fierce, especially on common keywords such as *"mutual funds"* where the top position might cost as high as $30 per click. You don't want to bid on high keywords; instead you may want to use alternate keywords like *"mutual funds diversification Chicago"* or *"financial advisor specializing in doctors San Antonio"*.

In a nutshell, you should try to think of specific and targeted keywords and go after them. As a result, instead of paying $30 for a keyword, you might end up paying 50 cents!

Great Resources

✓ Google Keyword Tool – allows you to plug in a URL and shows you what keywords Google thinks the page should be advertising for. Also shows keyword search volume estimates and keyword values...by keyword, site, or category.

- o https://adwords.google.com/select/KeywordToolExternal
- ✓ Google Traffic Estimator – estimates the number of Google AdWords ad clicks and bid prices for the top ad position.
  - o https://adwords.google.com/select/TrafficEstimatorSandbox

Social Media Gets in the PPC Game

Recently, the pay-per-click concept has crept into social media with sites like Facebook and LinkedIn offering opportunities to target ads to specific groups. This could be a more cost-effective way to place ads as it's possible to narrow the focus to occupational groups, regional locations, or people with shared interests.

LinkedIn DirectAds is a pay-per-click solution offered on LinkedIn. 25% of financial advisors who were surveyed on their LinkedIn use indicated that they had used DirectAds, and our own informal surveys indicate that most advisors are extremely satisfied with their results. The power of LinkedIn DirectAds lies in the way it allows you to drill down the 32 million U.S. based LinkedIn members and let you decide who you want to target. For instance, if you want to target attorneys you can narrow your ad placement to reach that specific audience, which numbered 670,000 as of August 2010. It's possible to drill down even further by specifying an age range, firm size, and geographic location.

It's worth a look if you're trying to develop leads for your products or services, and you're willing to invest some time and money. But, if your main objective is to increase brand awareness or expand your network of qualified prospects, you may be better off staying with the standard features of LinkedIn.

Converting Web Traffic Into Business Opportunity

The bulk of this book has focused on getting a web strategy in place to vastly expand your marketing reach and create the opportunity for people searching for financial solutions to find you. Its push-pull strategy consists of pushing your brand out to the internet and then letting your web apparatus pull the people in. With your website, social media, e-newsletter marketing, and blog all working in concert, the people who are driven to your website are more qualified to the extent that their visit is a strong indication of their need for financial solutions. So, how do you convert these visitors into business opportunities?

Add a Call to Action

When your website receives visitors the value of your web property increases. The more visitors, the more valuable it becomes. But, if your visitors are allowed to leave without giving them an opportunity to take some action, your website is as valuable as vapour. We've talked about the importance of engaging your visitors to keep them on your website. It is also essential to include a call to action that will move them a step further in your business development process. This can be as simple as including a registration box so they can opt-in to email updates. Other calls to action may include:

- ✓ E-newsletter opt-in
- ✓ Text Update opt-in
- ✓ Request for more information
- ✓ Client review request
- ✓ Invitation to join your social networks
- ✓ Seminar or webinar registration
- ✓ Tell a Friend

Not only do these calls to action move your visitors closer to business development opportunities, they enable you to collect valuable contact data. It is important to utilize an auto responder service that will generate automatic responses of acknowledgement. An auto responder will generate responses that are specific to the type of request.

Profitable Tip: Send a welcome email or letter to all of your clients and prospects inviting them to visit your website and register for your e-newsletter.

Invite Prospects to Take Action

People who roam the Web looking for answers to their financial questions tend to be open to new ways to learn about themselves and discover possible solutions. Anytime you can offer your prospects an opportunity to do so in an innovative way, you increase the chances of having them interact with your website and leave behind their contact information with permission to engage them.

EISI, a leading provider of financial planning software tools, has introduced a remarkable tool, Retirement CFA, that is designed to attract prospects to a simple self-directed assessment tool that enable them to easily model different financial strategies that apply to their financial situation. At the conclusion of their session, the prospect's contact and asset information are sent to you in an email and compiled in a lead database for contact purposes.

The application actually resides on a separate website that you customize with your color template and it can be linked to from your main website, social media outlets, email newsletters or blog. It was designed to integrate with EISI's financial planning software tools and its unique presentation tool which allows users to view the assessment results in a slide show. Of course, you need to already be

HERE'S WHAT A LETTER TO YOUR CLIENTS MIGHT LOOK LIKE.

Dear *CLIENT FIRST NAME*,

"I am writing you today to introduce my newly established website, www.mywebsite.com. Please take a moment to look it over, because I know you will find many valuable tools and resources to help you stay current on financial issues that matter to you. You'll also be able to check on the performance of your own portfolio.

You will also notice a tab called "Tell a Friend." CLIENT FIRST NAME, there's something I want to run by you. It's been my experience that about 20% of my clients will introduce me to friends, family, and colleagues without any encouragement from me. They do so because they enjoy the experience of working with me.

Another 20% or so don't like to make introductions like this. I guess they're just very private people who don't feel comfortable with that sort of thing.

And about 60% of my clients would be willing to introduce me to others, with my encouragement and with the proper means to do so.

The "Tell a Friend" link provides an easy way for you to introduce me in a simple, efficient, and unobtrusive way. It's really your way of saying "thanks MY NAME" and is, for me, the ultimate compliment.

Please take the time to consider this and help me grow my practice. I appreciate your loyalty, and I am thankful that someone once took the time to make your introduction."

Best Regards,
My Name

For electronic versions of this and additional templates and samples that may be most applicable for your practice visit our blog at www.advisorwebsites.com/blog .

Some additional tips:

- ✓ Each book of clients will be different , so you will have to assess whether they should receive a letter or an email. If using a physical mail-out letter, make sure you personally sign each letter.
- ✓ You will probably want to tweak the contents of the template to match your clients' profiles.
- ✓ You will probably get better results with a follow-up phone call after you send out your communication.
- ✓ Many advisors found success by demonstrating the "Tell a Friend" function to their clients even going as far as assisting them in filling it out. Oftentimes, your clients like to be guided by the hand in the referral process.

a user in order to add Retirement CFA, which is probably another good reason to consider EISI for your planning software needs.

Encourage Client Referrals

Your clients are always your best source of qualified prospects. One of the main reasons financial advisors don't receive more referrals is that they don't give their client the opportunity to help them. Even those advisors who faithfully ask their clients for referrals run into difficulty if they don't provide their clients with a process or the means to provide them. It's often left to the client to think of some people and then get back with the advisor in their own time, which is typically forever.

Install a Referral Template. Use your website to provide your clients with the tools to proactively promote you to their friends and colleagues. Your website has the capacity to store downloadable letter templates your clients can then customize and send via email or letter.

Don't expect your clients to access the template on their own. They will need some encouragement from you in the form of an email or letter that points them to the template. It's a great way to introduce your client to your new website, and those clients who have been willing to help you will be glad to have the means to do so. Advisors who have utilized this method report very favourable results.

Summary

If you have been a financial advisor for any length of time, you have probably devoted most of your marketing efforts to self-promotion, which included activities such as direct mail, seminar marketing, and networking. With a web strategy in place, you can let your web apparatus do the work for you so you can focus your efforts on business development and client relationship management.

As you launch your web strategy, you will need to shift your marketing efforts to web promotion, but once all of the pieces are in place, it propels itself. As the momentum of your web marketing efforts builds, your expenditure of time and resources will begin to decrease. As with any form of marketing, it is important to track and tweak to ensure you are achieving optimal results.

Web marketing is a constantly evolving discipline, with new technologies, applications and ideas emerging almost daily. You will be able to achieve greater efficiencies and results by keeping current with the latest marketing trends. Websites such as www.copyblogger.com and www.mashable. com are leading sites for staying on top of web marketing trends.

For more marketing ideas, resources and timely case studies dedicated to financial advisors, visit the Advisor Websites blog at www.advisorwebsites.com/blog.

CHAPTER EXERCISE

✓ Make a list of the 3 things you will implement this month that will help you market your website.

✓ Add a call to action to you website.

✓ Send out a communication to your clients about your website / social media profile / blog etc...

8   MONITORING AND MEASURING FOR RESULTS

"It's much easier to double your business by doubling your conversion rate than by doubling your traffic."

- Jeff Eisenberg

For financial advisors, there are two main business purposes for pursuing a web marketing strategy. The first is to improve their capacity to acquire new clients without which their business will not grow. The second purpose is to enhance their ability to retain their best clients and increase their value to the business. Without question, if your web strategy could accomplish both, it would be considered an undeniable success.

But how will you know if your strategy is working effectively toward those ends? A lot of time and resources could be expended before you determine that it is or isn't working, and even then you aren't likely to know the reasons. In marketing, it is critical to know the reasons behind the results so that productive activities can be repeated or expanded, and non-productive activities can be adjusted or eliminated.

Monitoring and measuring business or marketing activities is essential in order to achieve optimal results. The great advantage of web marketing is that there are a lot of built-in metrics that can be used to instantly tell you if it is working. And, because these can be tracked daily, you can see trends emerging that enable you to make adjustments so you can quickly change course.

Monitoring Activity and Measuring Results Always Improves Results

As a financial advisor, you know that if you uncover a certain number of new qualified prospects, a percentage of those will ultimately be converted into new clients. The challenge for most advisors has never really been to convert qualified prospects into clients; rather, it has always been to create a constant flow of qualified prospects, which is really the goal of your marketing efforts. The goal of a web marketing strategy should therefore be focused on generating a constant stream of visitor traffic from which a sufficient number of qualified prospects can emerge.

Can web marketing effectiveness therefore be measured simply by tracking the amount of traffic to your website? It may be a start, but it still relegates your web strategy to a pure numbers game. What if you could know which source of visitor traffic produced the most qualified prospects? Better yet, what if you were able to increase the number of visitors who are most likely to become qualified prospects? What if you were able to pinpoint which specific content component was attracting the most traffic? Would that increase your efficiency and your ROI? You bet.

**For the last time, no, I do not know
what the ROI is on it!**

Web Marketing Metrics for Financial Advisors

We were tempted to name this section, "Web Marketing Metrics for Dummies;" however, we will leave it to you to determine if that might be a good fit for you. While there are many tech-savvy financial advisors, most are not and have no real desire to be. Web analytics can delve pretty deeply into the weeds of your web performance, and it can be overwhelming, especially if you don't really know what to look for. We simplify the process here with a short list of the key metrics that can help guide you in your web marketing efforts:

Visitor traffic – this is a key indicator that tells you how many visits your website receives on a daily basis. Obviously, the more, the better.

Repeat visits – a rising number of repeat visits is an indication of your site's usefulness and popularity.

Page views – this tells you how many pages of content have been viewed by your visitors. Higher page views may indicate the level of interaction your visitors have with your website. Ultimately you want them to end up on a goal page like your contact page or an opt-in page.

Top pages – gives you an idea of which pages on your site are most popular. For many advisor websites we have found that one of the most popular pages include a biography page, which is a strong indication that your visitors are doing some serious research on you and your services. Well equipped resource pages that contain tools and article archives are also well traveled. Contact pages also receive a lot of views.

Visit duration – this is an important indication of how useful or engaging your visitors find your site. Short visit durations may be an indication of uninspiring content.

Timeline – while most metrics give you a snapshot of your website, a timeline history lets you see how they are trending. Timeline charts allow you to compare performance daily or monthly. This is useful when tracking marketing campaigns. i.e. If you send out communication to all your clients directing them to you site, you are likely to see a spike in the timeline.

Search term- this tells you what keywords your visitors are using to find your site in the search engines. If you find certain keywords being used more often, it may be a signal to find a way to work those keywords into more of your content which can get your site ranked higher for those keywords.

Referring Sites – this reveals the sites from where your visitors are coming. Common referring sites include search engines (like Google and Yahoo!), social networking sites (like LinkedIn.com, Twitter.com and Facebook.com), client sites, directories, and so forth. It can be a strong indication of how well your social media components are working in your overall web strategy.

Web Monitoring and Measuring Essentials

Web measurement and analytic tools are plentiful and many of the good ones won't cost you a dime. If your web marketing strategy has multiple media components, such as a website and some social media, you may need to deploy a few different measurement tools, but the great thing about most of them is that you just set it and forget it. The analytics will come to you via an email notification.

One of the problems of finding good analytic tools is that there are a plethora of choices. We've listed some of our favorite analytic tools here to help you narrow down the choices:

Web Analytics

Google Analytics - We personally utilize Google Analytics (www.google.com/analytics) and love its simplicity and its cost (free!). With just a couple of clicks it integrates itself with any website and then begins to pump out a tremendous amount of data and analytics on the site's performance. We rely upon three main reports that Google Analytics produces:

1. Traffic volume – how many visits, both unique and repeat
2. Traffic source – where our visitors come from
3. Visitor activities - what they do once they arrive on the site

Google Analytics produces a huge amount of data that, at some point, you may find useful. For those who want to be able to drill down some more, Google offers webinar courses through its university that can help you crank up your geek meter.

Website Grader - Website Grader (www.websitegrader.com) was developed by Hubspot.com as a website analyzer that will score your website in a number of usability and performance areas and then provide some recommendations for improving them. It weights the effectiveness of your content's readability, the site's SEO design, overall site structure, and its interaction with your social media websites. The feedback is well organized, very constructive, and it is geared toward helping you increase your site's visibility and traffic flow.

Social Media Analytics

Twitter Grader - If you use twitter, Twitter Grader (http://twittergrader.com/) is probably the most popular online tool for measuring the power, authority and reach of your tweets. It can let you know how you stack up as a Twit.

Facebook - Like the Twitter Grader, Facebook Grader (http://facebook.grader.com/) measures your reach, authority and popularity on Facebook. The score is based on the number of friends you have, and their power and influence as a network, and the completeness of your profile, among other things.

LinkedIn - Some social media sites can provide you with an indication of how users are interacting with your profile. A personal favorite is provided by LinkedIn, which allows you to see who's looked at your profile and how many times you have shown up in search results.

Postling.com - Postling.com is a clean and simple tracking tool that enables you to efficiently monitor all of your social media efforts and manage your online reputation through your email inbox. It tracks comments, replies, social streams, post updates, RSS feeds and keyword searches. Each day it sends you a digest of the prior day's activities from all of your social media sites. It also enables you to schedule and publish posts to your blog and all of your social media sites.

The True Measure of Your Success

Website traffic, views, hits, external links, visitor data and page rankings are all important factors for measuring the effectiveness of your website. But, it's important not to forget the reason for embarking upon your web marketing strategy. Ultimately, it is to increase your revenue which is a key measure of your success.

Your web marketing strategy is but one prong of your overall business plan, and if it is not producing the results you need to achieve your financial goal, and ultimately, your vision of overall success in your business life as well as your personal life, then adjustments need to be made. Establishing a clear vision and well-defined goals with measurable benchmarks are essential in order to measure the effectiveness of any strategy.

Ray Adamson, a strategic coach and consultant for the industry's top producers, reminds us that, without clearly defined financial goals, your chances of success are greatly diminished. By stating a specific number target, rather than a range or a percentage increase, your target is more easily segmented, by milestones, by source, by market, and by product, to allow for frequent measurement and assessment.

> *"Your plan is your roadmap to success. And that roadmap is a lot easier to follow when you know what your destination looks like. On the way to achieving your vision take stock of your goals, and your progress, regularly (at least on a quarterly basis) to ensure you are on the right track."*
> **Ray Adamson**

Summary

An effective web marketing strategy will generate a continuous stream of activity that will translate into more business opportunities that can then lead to increased revenue. Because there is usually a lag between marketing efforts and resulting business revenue, it is vital that these efforts be monitored and measured to ensure that they are on track to achieving their objectives.

A marketing strategy is not static. It usually requires constant adjustments and amendments in response to the fluidity of market conditions and consumer behaviours. The immediacy of data and analytics available to your web marketing efforts makes it possible to instantly know how they are working and why, enabling you to optimize your overall strategy.

CHAPTER EXERCISE

✓ If you have not done so, sign up for a free Google analytics account www.google.com/analytics and connect it with your website

✓ Check the statistics of your website/blog/social media sites/or the results of your latest campaign.

✓ Grade your web presence using these tools and consider any suggestions provided by these tools:

   o   Website: www.websitegrader.com

   o   Twitter: http://twittergrader.com/

   o   Facebook: http://facebook.grader.com/

9 YOU AND THE WEB – THE NEW COMPLIANCE FRONTIER

"Information on the internet is subject to the same rules and regulations as conversation at a bar."

- George Lundberg

Well, you knew it was coming, because it had to. After 8 chapters of unbridled discussion on advisor web marketing we are compelled to add this very important chapter on compliance, because to do otherwise would be both irresponsible and a disservice to you and your compliance departments.

By no means do we consider ourselves to be experts in compliance issues, so our purpose is not to offer any specific advice along these lines. However, based on our experience in working with advisors on website development, we can offer some observations and pass along some information that may be useful to you as you embark upon your web marketing strategy.

Obviously, the first and last word on the matter should come from your compliance department. Suffice it to say, your very next course of action should be to check in with your compliance department as it will save you a lot of time and resources.

God, I need an Advil.

Useful Observations, Information and Tips for Web Compliance:

Websites

Advisor websites have been in use within the financial services industry for several years and most broker-dealers have well-established policies that guide their use. Most advisors adopt a pre-fabricated, compliant website template provided by their broker-dealer or through a website provider. The issue with website content is handled much in the same way as any advertising content that requires pre-approval before it is published and archiving after its use.

The best way to minimize any potential compliance barriers is to work with a website provider that specializes in the financial services industry as they have already incorporated many of the compliance requirements and tools into their framework. It is especially important that your website includes archiving capabilities. You can find website providers that offer a substantial amount of customization that helps distinguish your brand.

Blogging

More financial advisors are catching on to the benefits of blogging as a way to boost their visibility and authority and, as a result it is receiving more attention from regulators and compliance departments. FINRA recently published its guidelines for the use of blogs and has, essentially found that blog posts are considered to be a form of advertising, so they need to follow the same review requirements as other forms.

This, according to some financial bloggers takes away from the spontaneity and timeliness of blog posts and can render them less interesting. While that may be true, blogging can still be a valuable tool for increasing your visibility, promoting your e-newsletter, and driving traffic to your website.   One tip, offered by several advisors is to create a batch of blog posts and have those all pre-approved so that these can be uploaded with greater frequency.

Email

Industry regulators have introduced stringent compliance archiving requirements regarding electronic communications in response to the explosive growth of email & instant messaging (IM) as principle business communication tools. Email can be legally admissible as evidence in court.

In many cases, advisors can utilize archiving technologies that enable them to rapidly produce evidentiary-quality email records with full audit trails on email and IM history.

Organizations like Global Relay (www.globalrelay.com) provide a range of products specifically engineered to meet the compliance archiving, monitoring, auditing, privacy and business continuity.

Social Media

Social media has drawn the most attention by regulators and compliance departments, largely because the number of financial advisors jumping on board has grown substantially over the last couple of years. Studies show that as much as 60% of financial advisors use social media in some way in their practice. The same studies show that nearly 40% of them are doing so without the approval of their compliance departments.[17]

Compliance departments have been slow to issue policies on the use of social media, but that is changing as a result of the FINRA guidelines that were released in early 2010. Broker-dealer firms must establish their own policies based on FINRA guidelines and advisors must refrain from using social media until they are in place.

One of the big issues keeping social media use at bay is the lack of archiving capabilities. Compliance departments aren't convinced that advisors can do this manually. Archiving solutions for social media are springing up that can possibly eliminate this roadblock. Social media archiving service, Arkovi offers a solution for financial advisors who need to be able to fully manage their social media footprint. Other technology vendors are developing company solutions that can help financial services firm manage security and control of social media use over their network.

17 Financial Advisor Magazine. "Financial Advisors Breaking Rules to Use Social Media". (Web. June 2010)

Ghostwriting

In Chapter 6 we did refer to ghostwritten articles as a content creating solution for advisors, so we wanted to briefly touch on ghostwriting compliance issues here. Ghostwriting is another area where FINRA has well-established policies in place through its regulatory notice 08-27, "Misleading Communications About Expertise"[18] , yet the web, with its self-publishing capabilities and the increased need for content, has heightened the issue and is worth revisiting.

Essentially, FINRA has said that any publication – article, newsletter, book, blog post – that is written by a person other than the advisor, must credit the person as the author. If advisors have no role in the creation of the content, their name cannot be included on the byline. If, however, they contribute in the way of a content outline or editorial direction, their name can be included on the byline.

Summary

When asked "what took you so long to get on the web", many financial advisors will point to compliance requirements and constraints as the reason. As more compliance departments answer the call to remove the barriers, advisors must look for other reasons or excuses for their web avoidance.

Web communications is a new frontier for the regulatory agencies and compliance departments, so advisors who want to blaze the trail need to exercise some patience while the policies and guidelines get mapped out. The only practical advice we'll offer is to stay in step with your compliance department and make yourself a part of the solution, not the problem. They call them as they see them and, whether you agree with the call or not, it is always the right one when it comes to protecting your practice.

18   http://www.finra.org/web/groups/inustry/@ip/@reg/@notice/documents/notices/p038522.pdf

CHAPTER EXERCISE

✓ Review your Broker Dealer / Head Office compliance guidelines related to a web presence.

✓ Consider an archiving solution if you are using Social Media. We like www.arkovi.com.

✓ Check to see if you have archiving capabilities on your current website. If not consider researching a provider that complies with FINRA/SEC regulations.

CONCLUSION

Compliance issues aside, the number one reason given by financial advisors for not implementing a web strategy is that they don't know how or where to get started. This lack of knowledge, when combined with the fear of being the newbie in the room, keeps most people out of the game. But, this is a game that you don't want to miss if you hope to compete in the new digital world.

Once you realize that everyone is new to this game (after all it's only been played for a few years) the intimidation factor should no longer hold you back. Even the so-called experts are still shuffling their way through the dark, progressing only through trial and error. The Web is in a constant state of flux with new technologies and applications emerging on a daily basis which makes us all newbies over and over again.

Take note: At the forefront of the evolving web landscape are the consumers, your prospects and clients, who now dictate through their behavior, desires and preferences, just how marketers are to treat them. Gone are the days when marketers controlled the message and how it was to be delivered. The 200 million U.S. consumers who spend an average of eight hours a week in the digital world, now control everything – the content of the message, how it is to be delivered, when it is to be delivered, how they will respond, and to whom they will respond.

Gone are the traditional marketing and prospecting ploys of direct mail and cold calls. Even "drip" marketing, the strategy of pushing out messages using various methods such as phone calls, emails, newsletters, and follow-up calls, has become passé as consumers now eschew the traditional methods of communications. In the book, *Sociable!*, the authors suggest that "reverse drip" marketing, using an apparatus of web and social media tools to draw consumers to you, capitalizes on the new methods of communication and engagement preferred by consumers.

Financial advisors who continue to expend resources on tracking down prospects in target markets and then pushing out boiler-plate messages where they aren't wanted are missing the whole point of web marketing. The internet has made it possible for advisors to simply cast out the right kind of bait that will attract type of prospects they want and then wait for them to latch on. While it doesn't happen overnight, at least the E-Advisors have immersed themselves in the same waters as the target market they are pursuing.

Financial advisors also must recognize that their clients, influenced by the empowering tools of Web 2.0 technology, have developed a whole new set of expectations for a professional relationship. Living in the digital world, they have become accustomed to having everything – information, communications, shopping, news dissemination, even their sports scores – totally customized to their preferences and priorities. Providing such a customized experience for all clients is beyond the realm of advisors without a web apparatus to support them.

Beyond the modernization of marketing, prospecting and relationship building methods, the Web offers financial advisors an opportunity to achieve something they all desire – stature and authority – without which they will not be able to effectively compete for affluent and wealthy investors.

The strategic application of a web apparatus consisting of a well-designed website, an authoritative blog, a social media presence and quality content can establish any financial advisor as an authority and elevate his or her stature and visibility within any targeted community. What once took many years of networking, scrounging for PR or speaking opportunities, and a fortune in advertising, can now be condensed into just a year or two at a fraction of the cost.

Seth Godin, dubbed "America's Greatest Marketer" and founder of Squidoo.com, expresses the urgency for taking action better than anyone:

> *"How can you squander even one more day not taking advantage of the greatest shifts of our generation? How dare you settle for less when the world has made it so easy for you to be remarkable?"*

WebVisor – The financial advisors guide to the internet, has laid it all out for you – the components, the tools, the best practices, the resources and the way forward. You now have the blueprint. Everything is at hand and nothing is beyond your capacity to implement a complete web marketing strategy. It's now up to you to create your vision of your practice in a digitally connected world.

CHAPTER EXERCISE

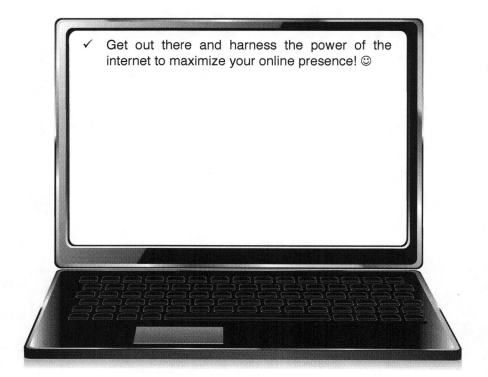

✓ Get out there and harness the power of the internet to maximize your online presence! ☺

ABOUT BART WISNIOWSKI

Bart Wisniowski is an entrepreneur and web development specialist committed to creating effective websites for professionals in the financial services industry.

Bart is the co-founder of Tidal Interactive (where he currently sits on the board of directors) and AdvisorWebsites. com (where his is actively involved in running the business), two highly successful web development firms. As a speaker at various conferences, training sessions, and industry events, he conveys the importance of having a professional online presence.

Bart's mission is to help financial advisors create effective, user-friendly, customized websites, and his company has a stellar track record for website development. He understands what financial advisors are looking for in a website to help them attract clients and build their business.

Bart received his bachelor of business administration from Simon Fraser University with a double concentration in Finance and Management Information Systems. He has been working in the web development industry since 2000 and exclusively with financial advisors since 2002.

In his personal life he likes to spend time with his family, is an avid winter activities participant and enjoys most team sports.

Bart is a member of the Financial Planning Association and is also a long time volunteer with his local Advocis chapter.

Email: bart@advisorwebsites.com
Personal Website: www.bartwisniowski.com
Twitter: @bartwisniowski
Linked In: http://www.linkedin.com/in/bartwisniowski

ABOUT JASON LINDSTROM

Jason Lindstrom is the managing partner at AdvisorWebsites.com where he manages product development and North American operations. Jason has over 10 years experience in the web development industry and has launched hundreds of web sites for the commercial, non-profit and financial sector.

Jason received an honors degree from Simon Fraser University in Communications and Publishing. During his academic career he was recognized as one of the top three entrepreneurs in Canada at the CIBC Student Entrepreneur of the Year Awards for founding Tidal Interactive where he acts as the President and CEO.

He is passionate about web usability and staying on top of the latest technical standards. Jason is a regular public speaker and likes to speak about both entrepreneurship and web usability.

Jason is married to Opi Lindstrom and loves skiing, cycling and swimming. Jason recently qualified and competed in the 2009 Triathlon World Championships in Australia.

Email: jason@tidal.ca
Twitter: @jasonlindstrom
Linked In: www.linkedin.com/in/tidalmedia

ABOUT ADVISOR WEBSITES

Since 2002, Advisor Websites has been assisting financial advisors in creating effective, compliant, and customized websites. No matter the size of your business, we can help you design and maintain a web site that fits your needs.

Our easy-to-use development process allows you to pick the framework elements and information you want without worrying about technical details. An account manager will guide you through the web development process and beyond, offering ongoing technical support, training & education even after your site goes live.

Visit us at www.advisorwebsites.com to find out more and to sign up for a free 30-day trial. Enter coupon code "WebVisor" to receive an additional month for only $1.

With Advisor Websites, you can look forward to:

- ✓ A free 30-day trial
- ✓ Customizable website templates and designs.
- ✓ No contracts or upfront fees
- ✓ Compatibility with many technology providers in the financial services industry
- ✓ An easy-to-use development process and technology platform
- ✓ Ongoing guidance from an account manager through-out the web development process
- ✓ Technical support after your site goes live
- ✓ Faster submission process with major compliance departments
- ✓ Great customer support

Twitter: @advisorwebsite
LinkedIn: www.linkedin.com/company/advisor-websites
Facebook: www.facebook.com/advisorwebsites

NOTES

11454909R00081

Made in the USA
Charleston, SC
26 February 2012